UNCOMMON ADVENTURES

A TRAVEL GUIDE TO THE JOURNEY OF FAITH

UNCOMMON ADVENTURES

A TRAVEL GUIDE TO THE
JOURNEY OF FAITH

MARK A. TABB

ISBN 0-8024-0727-7

Printed in the United States of America

To Ruth Smith,
who lived this book
long before I ever thought
of writing it

Contents

Acknowledgments

$\mathcal{T}$hank you to the four women in my life who patiently stood by me and encouraged me to never give up. To Bethany, whose name will someday top the best-seller list; to Hannah, who has never learned the word *impossible*; and to Sarah, who fills my life with joy and laughter— to my three daughters, thank you. To my loving wife, Valerie, who chased a dream with me across the country: Without you this would have been impossible. I love you very much. Thank you for believing in me.

I also want to thank Jim Bell of Moody Press for taking a chance on an unknown, first-time author. Thank you as well to Cheryl Dunlop, my editor at Moody, for your hard work on this project and for your patience with an overeager writer.

A special word of thanks to Marilyn Meredith, who helped me discover a passion for writing. Thank you for praying for this project for so very long. You made me believe that I could actually be a writer.

FOLLOW
ME

*F*ollow Me. He didn't say where they would go, and He never told anyone how long the trip would take. Only two words: Follow Me.

Two fishermen heard these words as they strained to drag in their nets filled with the morning catch. Brothers, business partners, they looked across the net to each other and simultaneously dropped that net to run up the beach after the one who called, "Follow Me."

A tax collector sat in his booth contemplating the price he continued to pay for his prized position with the Roman government. Since the day he purchased his "revenue franchise," his fellow Jews had shunned him. He embodied everything his countrymen hated about the Romans, and they despised him for it. Friends were plentiful—money always attracts friends—but they too were outcasts. Suddenly the noise of a crowd awakened him from his daydreaming. "Follow Me." He heard the man speak but couldn't believe He was talking to him. No explanation of where they would go was offered, only the command, "Follow

Me." The tax collector didn't hesitate. He left everything behind and followed.

A COSTLY CALL

News of the teacher spread throughout Judea like the sirocco winds that swept in from the desert in late spring. For one young man the reports sparked renewed hope deep inside his heart. Something was missing from his life, and he didn't know what or why. Never in his life had he lived without anything. His father gave him both wealth and prestige; the rabbis instructed him in the ways of God. He had it all, yet everything seemed hollow, empty. The nagging void grew until the day the teacher came through the young man's hometown. The young man ran to the traveling rabbi, fell to his knees, and cried out, "Good teacher, what must I do to inherit eternal life?"

The teacher looked at him and loved him. "Leave everything behind and come follow Me," He gently replied, "and you will have true riches in heaven" (see Mark 10:17–22).

It wasn't the answer the young man wanted. *Leave everything behind? Everything? For what? Where do You plan to take me? What guarantees do I have that the journey will be worth the price? Do You know who I am? Do You know the position my family holds in this community? Do You honestly expect me to walk away from all of this to wander around across the wilderness following You? Give me some other hope. Isn't there some other way?*

THE CALL TODAY

Follow Me. Jesus continues to call us with these same words. We've tried to invent more palatable ways to rephrase His call to appeal to modern audiences. We offer steps to peace with God, spiritual laws, and ways to have a full and meaningful life. But when we listen to the appeal of the man from Galilee, we only hear two words echoing across time and space, "Follow Me." All that it means to be a Christian is summarized within these two small words. They assume that each one of us is going the wrong way and that none of us, if left to ourselves, will ever correct our course. We need to turn around, to change directions. The Bible calls this repentance. No one will ever follow Christ without it.

To follow also means letting someone else lead, someone who

knows the way. Followers, those at the back of the line, don't shout out instructions for the leader to obey. Navigation is left to the one with the map, the person in the lead. On this journey, Christ not only sets the course, He also determines the pace. Every part of the trip is entrusted to Him. In a word, He is Lord. To believe in Him means to surrender to His lordship and follow Him wherever He may go.

But where is He going? Where will He take you and me if we decide to accept His offer and follow Him? Most of us would like some sort of road map, a travel guide to the journey of faith, for this trip is unlike anything we've ever experienced. We're following someone we cannot see to a place we know very little about. He takes us through unfamiliar territory without offering an explanation. And oh how we want an explanation. We continually try to figure out the big picture, His overall plan and direction for our lives. Jesus is content to reveal the road one step at a time. Where is He taking us? How long will this journey last?

No one can give you a detailed map of everything that lies ahead of you as you follow Christ. But I offer this work to you as a travel guide to let you know what to expect on the journey. Let me warn you, this isn't another book filled with advice of all you need to do to grow as a Christian. Rather, it is about what God plans to do in your life as He takes you from the initial step of trusting in His Son to the end of the journey: walking through the gates of glory. Though the journey moves us ahead and closer to the goal, we never really "arrive" at a destination. Our traveling focuses on several goals simultaneously. Interspersed with these are some unpleasant surprises and difficult paths we all must travel. In the pages that follow we will explore many of these.

We'll begin with the starting point of the journey, faith. Through the life of the prophet Jeremiah we will discover a picture of true, biblical faith. From far off we catch glimpses of a city on a hill and learn how to live to be comfortable as citizens in that city of holiness. The rest of our pilgrimage depends on developing this. Other destinations that lie ahead of us include spiritual maturity, ministry, and fellowship with the Lord Himself. A curious aspect of this journey is that we set off in pursuit of each destination simultaneously and yet never fully arrive at any in this life. But as we draw near we find ourselves being changed, becoming like the citizens of the cities we so desperately seek.

As we move on into the journey we will encounter some unpleasant traveling companions: gnats, gophers, and grizzly bears, trials that accompany everyone who makes the journey. We will also find ourselves on some difficult paths, including unanswered prayer and suffering. All along the way the bushes beside the road are filled with serpents, temptations that seek to offer what only appears to be good and end the expedition. Perhaps the most difficult aspect of the trek is its length. The road stretches on like an unending marathon, and even the most ardent of travelers can be tempted to give up. We will spend some time examining how and why this takes place.

Our travel guide finally arrives at our ultimate destination, heaven itself. The rest of the road may seem unclear, but we know without a doubt the ultimate prize God plans for His children. The hope of heaven's glory keeps us moving along when our legs are too weary to take another step. It lifts our sights above the troubles of today with the hope of everlasting glory.

After mapping out what lies ahead, we close with a discussion of what it takes to make the journey. By faith we take the first step onto this uncertain road, and by faith we continue traveling for a lifetime. As you will find, not everyone is willing to face the hardships of this trip. The two fishermen, Simon and Andrew, made the journey, as did Levi the tax collector. The rich young man decided the cost was too great and the road too uncertain. As you travel through the pages that lie ahead, you too will be confronted with a decision, a call from the Savior Himself. *Follow Me.*

Chapter One

THE FIRST STEP

*A*s if by habit his eyes strained to make out something, anything, but there was nothing to see. The only sounds were the rumbling of his stomach and the suction of the mud as he shifted his weight. He pressed his lips together as his tongue stuck to the roof of his mouth. All he could think about was water. "So this is the way it will end," he said to himself. "Stuck in the mud at the bottom of a well." Panic, anger, and despair had all come and gone. All he could do now was laugh.

His captors weren't laughing when they threw him here to die. Their voices burned with anger as they shouted, "Treason!" He'd been accused of many things, but being a traitor had never been one of them.

Doubt began to flood his mind in the darkness. *Maybe they're right. Listen to what you've been saying! How could you do such a thing?* He struggled to push the thoughts away by reminding himself he only repeated what he was told. These weren't his words; they came from God. The men up there were the real traitors. He'd kept himself pure; he'd stayed faithful. One final thought haunted him, *If that's true, what are you doing down here, Jeremiah? If God is on your side, why aren't you winning?*

THE STARTING PLACE

The bottom of a well is a strange starting point for any trip, especially a journey with the Lord. Our natural tendency is to assume that as long as Jesus Christ is captain of our lives everything will be smooth sailing. One view of the prophet waiting to die in the mud changes all that. His experience shows us what faith is all about. He grasped its essence and clung to it like a drowning man to a lifeline. Jeremiah never confused faith with positive thinking or optimism about the future. Nor did he ever consider it to be a path to material blessings and comfort, two things in short supply in Judah in 600 B.C. The prophet learned that faith means trusting God even when our experience tells us He is no longer trustworthy; entrusting ourselves to Him when reason cries out to do otherwise.

Jeremiah's adventure of faith began at an early age when God disrupted his life with these words: "Before I formed you in the womb I knew you, before you were born I set you apart; I appointed you as a prophet to the nations" (Jeremiah 1:5).

We all start at this same point. Granted, God doesn't usually visit while we're shaving and speak to us with an audible voice. But He does find a way to abruptly disrupt the flow of our lives and present us with a choice. His message is basically the same. He has a plan for our lives, a plan that will take a lifetime to complete. But completion won't come automatically. In fact, our natural tendency is to go in the opposite direction of His plan. Therefore we have to make a critical decision of whether to go our own way or follow His. Faith is choosing to take God up on His offer and follow Him.

Jeremiah didn't jump at the chance to change careers and follow God. He responded like any rational human: "Are You sure about this, God? I don't know how to speak. I'm only a child. Isn't there someone else who could do a better job?" Perhaps he hoped to have better results than Moses did when he argued with God at the burning bush. But God doesn't make mistakes. He reached out and placed His Word in the mouth of His new spokesman and gave him this guarantee:

"Today I have made you a fortified city, an iron pillar and a bronze wall to stand against the whole land—against the kings of Judah, its officials, its priests and the people of the land. They will fight against you but will not overcome you, for *I am with you* and will rescue you," declares the Lord. (Jeremiah 1:18–19, italics added)

Jeremiah faced the choice we all face when God speaks. We can either believe God and do what He asks, or we can ignore Him and go back to business as usual. This isn't just a choice that future prophets, pastors, or missionaries face. The call of Jesus Christ in the gospel is as radical as the call Jeremiah received 2,600 years ago. Jesus told the woman caught in adultery to leave her life of sin; the rich young ruler was told to sell everything that he had and give it to the poor; a Pharisee was told to go so far as to love a Samaritan, which would be comparable to a Serb being told to love a Bosnian. To believe in Jesus means to drop everything else to follow Him. There is no in-between. Jeremiah chose to take God at His word and follow Him. His adventure had just begun.

Armed with the promises of God, filled with His Spirit, and full of youthful determination, Jeremiah set out to change a nation. No doubt dreams of glory danced in his head. In his mind's eye he could see the wicked king of Judah tearing his clothes in mourning over the nation's sin. Surely his words would cut deep into the hearts of the corrupt religious establishment whose lives were a disgrace to the name of God. Idols would be smashed, lives would be changed. Everything seemed possible with the help of the Lord.

But things didn't turn out the way Jeremiah expected. He soon discovered that the path of faith is anything but predictable. The instructions he received from God bordered on the unbelievable, and the results he saw were far from what he had expected. He never experienced things we take for granted: family, home, security. He was thrown into prison on several occasions and died a captive of the exiles in Egypt.

NOT ALWAYS A PLEASANT HIKE

Jeremiah's experience helps us know what to expect when we

decide to walk by faith and follow Jesus Christ. We can expect the unexpected. Faith often leads us to places we do not want to be. Only a fool would suppose that the prophet enjoyed being thrown into an abandoned well or being carried off to Egypt with a group of rebels, but that's where his obedience to God took him. Jeremiah complained that he couldn't become a prophet because he was only a child. But God filled him with an amazing boldness. When they burned his writings, he wrote them again. False prophets slandered him to win the king's favor, but he kept right on preaching. Even though he wanted to give up many times, he never did.

Jeremiah wasn't some sort of spiritual superman. He had discovered one of the most surprising aspects of faith: The one who really acts on our faith is God, not us. We persevere not because our faith is strong but because God is faithful. As we entrust Him with our lives, He will not disappoint us. He carries us through impossible situations and does things through us that leave us shocked and amazed. All along the way we'll find that we can't take credit for anything. The praise and glory go to God alone.

Jeremiah's life also shows that faith doesn't guarantee happy endings. By the standards of the world he was an abysmal failure. We're not used to that. A hero doesn't fail—he rides off into the sunset after locking up the bad guys and winning the heart of the most beautiful girl in town. But this prophet failed. His books were burned, his sermons were ignored. His ministry produced a grand total of zero converts. By every standard of success he failed, and failed miserably. If not for the book that bears his name he might well have slipped into oblivion as if he had never lived.

DIFFICULT COMMANDS, LIMITED SUCCESS

We find the same drama being played out across the pages of both testaments. Noah was the only righteous man of his generation. What did God tell him to do? Build a boat miles from the sea before the first rains had ever fallen upon the earth. I doubt if he expected those kinds of instructions. He spent 120 years preaching from the pulpit of a giant ship. While gathering animals he continued to sound the warning that God's judgment was coming. No one listened. Everyone thought he was an eccentric old man building boats that would never float. When the day came to enter the ark only his family believed what he said.

Abraham also found favor in God's eyes. In fact, God loved him so much that He told him to leave home and travel two thousand miles to a special place, a place Abraham knew nothing about until the day he arrived. But God had more, much more, in store. The Lord made a promise to Abraham (who was then Abram), telling him he would soon have a son. Abram was seventy-five years old at the time and must have had a little trouble believing his ears. Little did he know that another twenty-five years would pass before he would hold his child for the first time. Then God topped all His other surprises by ordering Abraham up Mount Moriah so that he could sacrifice his long-awaited child. To say this came as a surprise is an understatement.

In spite of all of his obedience and faith, Abraham failed by the standards we use to judge our own success. Although he had been promised a nation, a tomb was the only land he ever owned. God promised him cities, but he lived in a tent all of his life. He was told that his descendants would outnumber the stars, but he did not live to see it. Yet he never wavered; he believed God would make good on His promise.

Moses was another of God's surprise packages. Who could doubt that God has a sense of humor when He arranged to have the deliverer of a nation of slaves raised in the household of the king? His life is so familiar that we lose the impact of the instructions God gave him. Think about what must have gone through his mind at the burning bush when God told him to go attack the mightiest nation on earth armed only with a shepherd's staff. No wonder Moses argued. It was the only sane response. He must have been shocked when the stick worked and he won!

If this were a movie, the picture would fade as Israel marched out of Egypt and into Canaan as conquerors. What could possibly go wrong? God had revealed Himself with power. The people committed themselves at Sinai to obey everything the Lord commanded them. Moses had succeeded. He had completed one of the most difficult assignments any man had ever been given.

Unfortunately the story does not end this way. The children of Israel soon wanted to go back to Egypt. Time after time they tested God's patience until finally they stepped over the line.

Only two of the adults who marched out of Egypt under Moses' leadership lived to enjoy the riches of the Promised Land. Today we would say that Moses had a knack for reaching people but he had problems with retention. His life's work seemed to be wasted in the sands of the desert where he died, never stepping foot into the land he spent a lifetime longing for.

The apostle Paul knew a little about encountering the unexpected. Sprinkled among his success stories of souls being saved were shipwrecks, imprisonment, attacks by angry mobs and hungry beasts, beatings, stonings, and hunger. At the end of his life he found himself alone in spite of all the lives he had touched with the gospel.

Being two thousand years removed from the most recent Bible characters, it is easy to forget that they went through such trials as real, flesh-and-blood human beings. Each of those mentioned has taken on legendary status in the eyes of the faithful. We often see them as a cross between John Wayne, Indiana Jones, and a Timex watch. They seem bigger than life, fearless, able to take a licking and keep on ticking. They were able to keep a stiff upper lip through every unhappy ending or unreasonable demand on their lives.

But disappointment and pain were no easier for a prophet or an apostle than for a plumber, doctor, mother, or father today. The heroes of old didn't enjoy pain. Paul never told God, "Keep it coming, Lord, I'm starting to like prison food." The pain they felt was real, and their disappointment with God was just as devastating then as now.

Despair and Anguish

Perhaps Jeremiah was the most human of them all. He knew all too well that failure breeds desperation and despair. Complicating matters was his intense love and compassion for the people of Judah. Many times he cried out, "O my Comforter in sorrow, my heart is faint within me. . . . Since my people are crushed, I am crushed; I mourn, and horror grips me. . . . Oh, that my head were a spring of water and my eyes a fountain of tears! I would weep day and night for the slain of my people" (Jeremiah 8:18, 21; 9:1).

This is not the picture usually painted of one of God's chosen vessels. It is difficult to believe that one who was supposed to be a giant of the faith could struggle with such pain. Yet time only intensified his anguish.

The anguish of his soul finally pushed him to the breaking point until he began to question God's justice. Everything was not turning out for the best. Life was not a sweet rhapsody of fellowship with a loving Lord. Instead, the wicked were prospering. The lying prophets who surrounded the king had great influence and enjoyed his favor. Jeremiah screamed for justice to be done. He cried out that at long last God would vindicate him. He'd gone as far as he could; now he was giving up.

The Lord's answer is surprising. Rather than comforting His chosen spokesman, the words God spoke seem to lack compassion: "If you have raced with men on foot and they have worn you out, how can you compete with horses? If you stumble in safe country, how will you manage in the thickets by the Jordan?" (Jeremiah 12:5). God offered no relief, only the assurance that things would grow more difficult. The trials which lay in the future dwarfed those of the past. A grim prospect indeed.

Why keep trying, then? Who wants to believe in a God who fills lives with pain and unhappiness? Jeremiah kept trying because he knew what Noah and Abraham had learned before him. He was sustained by the promise that had given Moses the strength to lead a group of rebels through the desert for forty years. It was the same revolutionary truth that gave Paul the courage to endure years of hardship for the sake of Jesus. This same timeless promise is what makes the struggle worth the effort today.

Faith doesn't guarantee fortune and fame. It has nothing to do with comfort and happiness. Rather, faith has everything to do with entering into a relationship with God, who far surpasses all of these. Jeremiah learned that by faith an ordinary man can enter into an extraordinary relationship with a loving God. As he struggled in the mud at the bottom of the well, that was all he had. But he knew that God was all he needed.

Foundational Faith

What we find in Jeremiah is a very simple definition of faith. It begins with the conviction that God is God. This sounds so elementary that it hardly warrants being said. But I find it amazing how often we forget this foundational truth. Faith begins with realizing that God is God and I am not. He is the center of the universe. Everything finds its meaning and purpose in God's design, not in how it can serve me. He created me for His good pleasure. He doesn't exist to serve me or to make my life merry and trouble free.

The New Testament completes this statement by telling us that Jesus is Lord. Paul captured the essence of Jesus' lordship in the first chapter of his letter to the Colossians.

> He is the image of the invisible God, the firstborn over all creation. For by him all things were created: things in heaven and on earth, visible and invisible, whether thrones or powers or rulers or authorities; all things were created by him and for him. He is before all things, and in him all things hold together. And he is the head of the body, the church; he is the beginning and the firstborn from among the dead, so that in everything he might have the supremacy. (Colossians 1:15–18)

Look at who Jesus is. He owns everything, He created everything, He holds everything together. All of creation yields to His sovereignty so that in everything "He might have the supremacy." No wonder Thomas fell at His feet and confessed, "My Lord and my God."

If Jesus is Lord, then He is also in control of everything that happens. The God of the Bible doesn't wring His hands over problems. His hair hasn't turned gray worrying over the messes we get ourselves into. The Lord is sovereign; He's in control. All of creation, visible and invisible, must obey His voice. If God is sovereign over creation, then we know that He is in control of our lives. Nothing that happens to an individual takes Him by surprise. On the contrary, He has a plan for my life and for yours.

This would be a frightening prospect without the assurance that God loves us. If we ever doubt this fact all we need to do is look back at the Cross. "But God demonstrates his own love for us in this: While we were still sinners, Christ died for us" (Romans 5:8). Faith isn't some mystical force that puts us in contact with a God far away in heaven. It is a response to a God who loves us so much that He gave His Son to die on our behalf. Though our sin demands that we die, Jesus died in our place that He might bring us to God. The maker and sustainer of all creation voluntarily died in our place. Why would He pay such a price? Because He loves you and me.

God's love doesn't stop on the cross. It determines how He relates to us forever. The Bible compares it to the love parents have for their children. This love assures us that God knows and does what is best for each of us. Don't misunderstand what I am saying. Our desires don't dictate to God what He must do. He isn't like a haggard mother running around trying to satisfy a spoiled child. Rather, God does what is best according to His eternal purpose, a purpose that elevates Jesus Christ and makes Him supreme in all things. Because God created you and me to know Him and glorify Him, our greatest happiness and greatest good come when we live in accordance with God's design and purpose.

Perhaps it was in the well that Jeremiah composed the words of one of my favorite passages in all of the Bible, Lamentations 3:19–24.

> I remember my affliction and my wandering,
> the bitterness and the gall.
> I well remember them, and my soul is downcast
> within me.
> Yet this I call to mind
> and therefore I have hope:
> Because of the Lord's great love we are not consumed,
> for his compassions never fail.
> They are new every morning;
> great is your faithfulness.
> I say to myself, "The Lord is my portion;
> therefore I will wait for him."

Whether in the well or sitting in a jail cell smelling the smoke of his life's work being burned, he had hope. Amazing. When he had nothing else, God's unchanging love sustained him. This is true faith. This is the first step of a lifelong adventure.

Travel Log:

*1. What do you expect from God? Before you give me the standard Sunday school answer, I want to probe a little deeper. As you follow Jesus by faith, or as you wrestle with making that decision, what kind of changes do you think He will make in your life?*_____

_____

Are there problem areas you hope He will fix? Are there strained relationships you want Him to restore? Have you been wrestling with failure that you want Him to transform into success? _____

_____

Deep down, do you expect God to make life easier and more enjoyable? Let's be honest before God. What do you truly expect God to do for you if you follow His Son by faith? _____

_____

2. When God speaks we face a choice. Either we can drop everything and follow Him, or we can ignore Him and hope He will leave us alone. We may not phrase our options in exactly these words, but this is truly the choice we face. What has God asked you to do that has disrupted the normal flow of your life? _____

_____

Don't confine this question to some mystical experience where God calls out to you with an audible voice. His Word is filled with commands, many of which are difficult to obey. Which ones trouble you the most? Are there any that you avoid because the voice of conviction is too great? _____

_____

What keeps you from obeying them? _____

3. The stories of Jeremiah, Noah, Abraham, and Paul may have brought back some painful memories. You may be able to relate well to them for you too have suffered through failures as a result of following the Lord. What effect did that experience have on your will-

ingness to trust God? _____

_____

Which of His promises brought you the greatest comfort in the midst of that storm? _____

_____

It could be that none of the promises brought you much comfort. Is there any unresolved anger and bitterness toward God that you need to stop now and resolve? _____

The wonderful thing about our God is that His compassions truly do not fail. Even at our lowest point, when all hope is lost and we are filled with despair, He is still on His throne and His love for us continues undiminished. You can come back to Him and set out again on this wonderful, uncommon adventure.

Chapter Two

THE CITY
SET ON
A HILL

*I*t's time now for a little quiz. What do the following items all have in common?

A day
A mountain
A plot of ground around a bush
A tent
A golden box
Incense
Oil
Custom-made garments
A city
A building
Loaves of bread
The Old Testament nation of Israel
You and me

Do you see a connection? As strange it as it may seem, one common thread ties them all together. God set each one of them apart at different times in history for His purpose and His glory. He considered every item on this list to be holy.

BIBLICAL HOLINESS

Holiness is perhaps the most important lesson God has for us on our journey of faith. Like the first answer in a long mathematics equation, every other step depends upon mastering this. If we miss it, we probably won't arrive at any of the others.

Yet we struggle to understand where God is taking us, for we don't fully understand what holiness is. The very mention of the word conjures up some timeworn, preconceived ideas. Usually we associate it with abstaining from sinful activity. Holy people don't smoke, drink, cuss, chase women, go to movies (at least dirty ones), or steal. Instead they spend all their time reading the Bible, going to church, and praying for missionaries. Or, we think of holiness as synonymous with serious and *boring*. We see holy people as starched-shirt Puritans walking around with glum looks on their faces. The slightest smile might cause their faces to crack. Not that they would actually *want* to smile. They're so preoccupied with trying to stamp out sin in the world that they don't have any time left to enjoy life.

If that's what holiness means, I don't want to go there. God is holy, but I can't imagine Him sitting around heaven looking glum and serious all day. Nor can I accept a definition of holiness that confines it to *not* doing something. My cocker spaniel doesn't smoke, cuss, or drink. Yet I doubt God had her in mind when He commanded you and me to be holy in all we do. And He does command us to be holy. Peter repeats the command God gave to Israel when he writes, "But just as he who called you is holy, so be holy in all you do; for it is written: 'Be holy, because I am holy'" (1 Peter 1:15–16).

What does it mean to be holy? The quiz we just took gives us a key. In and of itself none of the items stands out as extraordinary. We would pass all of them by without a thought, except that the Bible tells us that something about them is different. Although many of them started out plain and ordinary, *they became holy when God set them apart for His purpose and His glory*. He placed His name on them and declared, "This one is mine; I have something special in store for it." To be holy is to be set apart.

HOLY, NOT COMMON

The seventh day of the week was like any other day. The sun rose and the sun set. But when God rested on that day, He set it apart as different, as holy. Mount Sinai was nothing more than a pile of volcanic rocks in the desert until God set it apart as the place where He would meet with Moses and give Israel the law. And you and I are just like everyone else in this world until the moment we surrender our lives to Jesus Christ. At that point in time a dramatic transformation takes place. God sets us apart as His own special possession. Then we become saints—literally, holy ones—those who have been set apart from the rest of humanity.

When God sanctified something as holy, the way it was to be treated radically changed. The Old Testament law strictly prohibited taking something God set apart and using it for a common or profane purpose. The Tent of Meeting, the tabernacle, could not be rented out for weekend camping trips. Although it was a tent, it was different from the rest of the tents of Israel. Only God could dwell within it. The articles in the holy tent also changed. No one would think of using the ark of the covenant, the golden box holding the Ten Commandments, as a place to store old clothes. Holy things stood out from everything else as unique and different. Even though many of them started out as ordinary, when God chose them they became extraordinary. Never again could they return to the world of the commonplace.

Why? Because holy things draw their distinction from the one who claims them for His own. The temple was a holy building because it belonged to a holy God. From Genesis to Revelation, the Bible lifts up holiness as the essence of God's being. When we are allowed a glimpse of Him in heaven, He is always surrounded by a choir of angels singing out, "Holy, Holy, Holy is the Lord God almighty." He stands apart from all of creation. Nothing is like Him. All creation bears the stain of sin; but God is light and in Him there is no darkness at all. The physical universe began at a specific point in time and suffers from decay; but God is eternal and unchanging. All that exists is finite; God the Creator of heaven and earth is infinite. He is holy, set apart, enthroned over all of the universe.

HOLY IN CHRIST

All of this moves from being a religious word game to a life-changing experience when we notice that you and I are on God's special list of things He has set apart. Hebrews 10:10 states that we have been made holy by the once-for-all sacrifice of Jesus Christ upon the cross. In 1 Corinthians 6 Paul lists numerous vices that characterize the worst of sinners. He concludes this list with the words, "and that is what some of you were. But you were washed, you were sanctified [literally, made holy], you were justified in the name of the Lord Jesus Christ and by the Spirit of our God" (v. 11). In and through Jesus, God sets us apart and declares that we are already holy before Him. As hard as it is to imagine, when God looks at us He no longer sees the lies we've told or the property we've stolen. He sees only the righteousness of Christ enveloping us like pure, white garments.

This is only part of the equation. Although God has made us holy in Christ, He still calls us to *act* holy in the midst of the sinful world in which we live. In his opening statement to the church in Corinth, Paul reminded them that they were "called to be holy." Few cities in the ancient world could compare to the wickedness of Corinth. Sensuality permeated every aspect of its society. Yet even there God's people were called to be set apart, different, holy. Holiness is to be a way of life.

HOLY FOR A PURPOSE

Being holy is the essence of the Christian life. Again, it is more than *not* doing something. *God sets us apart for a specific purpose.* Remember Paul's words to the church in Ephesus where he said, "For we are God's workmanship, created in Christ Jesus to do good works, which God prepared in advance for us to do" (Ephesians 2:10). The Lord never set anything apart to sit on a celestial knickknack shelf as a conversation piece for the heavenly hosts. He always has a specific purpose in mind. Living according to God's purpose is living a holy life.

What possible purpose could God have in mind for you and me? Usually we get so hung up on looking for something specific, like *Should I buy the blue shirt or the pink one?* that we lose sight of His overarching plan for every believer. We think of

God's purpose and plan as a hidden mystery, but it is right before our eyes. Do you see it? Instead of looking up, look down and around. Have you noticed the condition of the world around us? Everywhere we look the darkness of sin reigns. Violence fills the streets of our cities, more than one million babies a year die at the hands of abortionists, illicit sex is a way of life. Do you see it now? God wants us to be salt and light in this world, a city set on a hill, in order that those who are trapped in the darkness of sin can come into the glorious light of the presence of Jesus Christ. In a nutshell, this is His purpose for our lives.

Being holy sets us apart from the world, but it doesn't disengage us from the world. True holiness makes a difference in the lives of those around us as well as in our own. It draws people toward God. I know this doesn't fit our stereotype of holiness. We're so afraid of being "holier than thou" that we forget who our example is. Was anyone holier than Jesus? He was the very embodiment of holiness, for He was God in human flesh. But I have yet to find a case where Jesus was too holy to associate with sinners. The Gospels paint a very different picture. Because Jesus was holy He could see the sin of those around Him so clearly that He had to do something about it. Rather than condemn, He offered people a way out.

As we arrive at the destination, holiness will move us to imitate Christ. His compassion for sinners will grow within us as we become more and more set apart to Him. Rather than looking down our noses at the world, we'll be moved to act. No one will have to convince us that this is His purpose for our lives. Soon it will become the primary thing we want to do. The holier we become, the more we'll long to be like Christ and "seek and save those who are lost." It will permeate every part of our lives. Paul was holy. He counted everything else in life as nothing more than garbage in comparison to knowing Christ and pursuing His purpose for his life. Have I done the same? The question haunts me even as I write these words.

Pursuing God's purpose comes at a price, the price of anonymity. Holiness doesn't leave any room for superstars, for it means being set apart to God for His purpose and *His glory*. Everything we do should exalt Jesus Christ and draw attention to Him. When we set out to live a holy life, this becomes our motivation in everything we do. We don't want to draw attention to ourselves; we aren't working for the applause of the crowds. Being holy means adopting the philosophy of John the Baptist: "He must become greater; I must become less" (John 3:30). When we are set apart for God's glory, we lose ourselves in Him.

HOLINESS AND SUFFERING

Making all this become a reality in our day-to-day life is not an easy process. In fact, it is very painful. Becoming holy produces suffering in the lives of God's children—not an external sort of agony thrust upon us by those who oppose God, but a pain that wells up from within us as the remnant of sin in our flesh fights for its survival. This is the reason the New Testament is filled with bloody and painful words to describe a life of following Christ. Here are just a few examples:

> If anyone would come after me, he must deny himself and take up his cross and follow me. (Matthew 16:24)

> Those who belong to Christ Jesus have crucified the sinful nature with its passions and desires. (Galatians 5:24)

> Put to death, therefore, whatever belongs to your earthly nature: sexual immorality, impurity, lust, evil desires and greed, which is idolatry. Because of these, the wrath of God is coming. (Colossians 3:5–6)

Look carefully at the imagery these words create. Put to death, crucify, take up your cross. Each one describes torment and pain. So often we read over these words as though carrying them out is as easy as putting on a fresh suit of clothes. All we need do is decide to do it and the task is over. I wish things could be so simple.

The writers of the New Testament chose this group of words carefully, because no others can adequately describe the pain that comes as we allow God to put our old man to death so that we can share in His holiness. One word captures the essence of this process: crucify. Unlike modern methods of execution, crucifixion was designed to be cruel and unusual punishment. The cross did more than punish with death. It sought revenge for all the wrongs the condemned criminal had ever carried out. Death came slowly, often waiting several days before it would take its victim. No one died defiantly on the cross, rebellious to the end like James Cagney in an old gangster movie. Those who were crucified suffered every sort of physical and emotional pain imaginable, breaking the spirit as well as the body.

HOLINESS AND HUMAN PRIDE

Crucifying our old nature produces the same sort of pain. It is a slow, grueling, and agonizing process. The pain afflicts the soul, striking at the very core of who we are. God drives the nails into our flesh as we plead with Him to set us free from sin. Our spirit rejoices at the news and in the freedom that results. But the old man, the sinful nature, cries out in agony. So often his cries draw our attention and we return to that place of crucifixion, caressing the flesh and trying to pull it down from the cross. Why else do we find ourselves constantly returning to old sinful habits that God has freed us from in the past? Why else do we entertain thoughts that have no place in our minds? We're caught like a rope in a tug-of-war between who we are in Christ and who we were in the flesh. The pain of watching the old man die can be excruciating.

What makes this so painful is the archenemy of holiness that dwells deep within our being: pride. It is what makes the process of dying to self so difficult: Before we can die to ourselves it must first be sacrificed. Before Jesus called His disciples to take up their crosses and follow Him, He commanded them to deny themselves. Pride and holiness are mutually exclusive terms. Thus, it should come as no surprise that this is one of the primary areas of our lives that God allows difficulties to tear down in the process of conforming us to His image.

Rare is the individual who doesn't wrestle with pride. It is both a root cause of sin and the very essence of rebellion. Isaiah captured its essence in this taunt against the king of Babylon,

> You said in your heart, "I will ascend to heaven;
> I will raise my throne above the stars of God;
> I will sit enthroned on the mount of assembly,
> on the utmost heights of the sacred mountain.

I will ascend above the tops of the clouds;
I will make myself like the Most High." (Isaiah 14:13–14)

The king of Babylon's words sound very much like those of Adam and Eve when they faced the first temptation. They yielded so that they too could be like God. When presented with the choice of humbly accepting their position as creatures before the Creator or trying to subvert His sovereignty, they chose the latter. From that day until now, pride has continued to wreak havoc on the human condition.

Pride makes us do some very strange things. Out of pride a man will drive miles and miles without a clue as to where he is or how to get where he wants to go, rather than stop and ask directions. Under the influence of pride we'll walk away from a friendship or a marriage rather than admit that we were wrong. Prejudice, envy, and hatred are all spawned deep within the recesses of our hearts from the seedbed of pride.

Yet believers in Jesus Christ are called to lay all that aside. In our relationship with God we're commanded to deny ourselves (Matthew 16:24), humble ourselves (Matthew 23:12), and consider all things loss in comparison to knowing the Lord (Philippians 3:7–8). As if this isn't hard enough, the Lord goes on to tell us to honor one another above ourselves (Romans 12:10), submit to one another (Ephesians 5:21), forgive one another (Matthew 18:21–35), and serve one another (Galatians 5:13). The final blow comes when the Lord addresses our relationship to ourselves. We're told to place no confidence in the flesh (Philippians 3:3) and to deflate our egos (Galatians 6:3).

Ideally, we'll do all of the above on our own. The Holy Spirit works through the Bible to prompt us to strip off our pride, and we obey. Unfortunately, things rarely turn out according to the ideal. Our egos stubbornly refuse to go down without a fight. Though we hear the clear message of Scripture, we have difficulty putting it into practice. We often fall into the trap of the Pharisees, becoming puffed up and proud over the meager success we have in following the Lord. As unlikely as it seems, we become proud of our humility.

What choice then does a loving God have but to help us along the way by striking a fatal blow to our vanity with adversity? On the surface such an act seems cruel and unloving. In reality it is an expression of pure love. Because our pride drives us away from the Lord and into the arms of sin, God allows difficulties and setbacks to afflict us. From a business failing to a child rebelling, trials have a way of humiliating us and taking away the pride that causes us to stumble.

The Priority of Holiness

Several years ago I learned this lesson the hard way. I was convinced all Christians should live completely debt free. Borrowing money wasn't even an option. Through our first four years of marriage my wife and I never used credit, a sterling record I was very proud of. Not only was I convinced that we should live this way, I believed my friends needed to come to the same conclusion. Debt-free living became my standard of spirituality and holiness.

Fortunately, God loved me enough to do something before I drove all my friends away. I had declared that I would never go into debt to buy a car no matter what. Thus God allowed us to keep a car we had so proudly paid cash for a few years earlier into the twilight of the car's life. First, the transmission died. Then the speedometer stopped at 99,999 miles. The headliner dropped, the air conditioner stopped cooling, the power door locks stopped locking. Finally, the timing chain broke and the car stopped running completely. The mechanic who revived it informed me that the engine itself would soon need to be replaced.

I found myself sitting alone in the kitchen one night, looking at the repair bills that had been rolling in, and I came to a stark discovery. I was indeed in debt with nothing to show for it. Though I wasn't making a car payment to GMAC, I was paying the mechanic nearly three hundred dollars a month to keep my broken-down old car on the road. But with the mechanic's bills and the ever falling gas mileage, there was no money left over each month to save for a new car. God had placed my pride on a plate and was serving it to me a piece at a time, not out of spite but out of love. What kind of car I own and how it is paid for means less to God than the condition of my heart. A heart filled with self-righteousness is a much greater offense in the eyes of

God than all the debt I could possibly amass. In the process of striving to be holy I had fallen into one of the worst forms of ungodliness. God used a very simple trial, constant car troubles, to expose this sin and root it out.

I know that I'm not alone. King Nebuchadnezzar was rendered temporarily insane, becoming more like an animal than a man because of his pride. Only after his pride was broken was he able to come to his senses and give God the glory and the credit for all He had done. Peter was humiliated on the night he denied Jesus three times. After the cock crowed and his eyes met those of his Lord, all of his stubborn resolve to follow Jesus even unto death melted away in a sea of tears. The man we find walking with Jesus along the Sea of Galilee after His resurrection is a broken and humble Peter who was now ready to glorify the Lord. In the same way, God loves us enough to break our pride to make us usable and holy.

Some of the pain of becoming holy comes through the trials that getting rid of our sin produces. Yet most of the trials we face as Christians do not come as a result of sin. Job's comforters made the terrible mistake of attributing his suffering to some hidden vice in his life. But Job wasn't going through the agony of judgment. His trial came from another source. God sometimes uses suffering to bring about holiness in the lives of His people. He is able to take what Satan intends as a way of driving people away from God and use it as a means to conform them to His image.

Holiness and the World

Adversity drives a wedge between the Christian and the world. By this I am not referring to the people of the world but the things of the world. In the midst of suffering, all the empty amusements and obsessions that people spend so much of their time and resources pursuing lose their luster. When tragedy strikes we stop caring about who will win the World Series or whether our favorite television show will return next season. We realize for perhaps the first time that these things really don't matter. New cars and diamond rings are worthless when someone we love is locked in a life-and-death struggle with cancer.

In these moments we find that we are able to share God's perspective on the things of the world. Life comes to a standstill in the midst of the struggle, and our eyes are opened. No wonder lives are changed after a close brush with death. Even the most ungodly of people, those who have no fear of God, get a new perspective on life when tragedy comes close to home. How much more so should those who are walking with the Lord?

Adversity weans us away from the amusements of the world and forces us to cling to the Lord. In the hour of trouble He is all that we have. We huddle up close to His side and cry out for His mercy. No one is able to go into the presence of God and emerge unchanged. When we are forced into His presence under the fire of suffering, we find that we will come out more like Him with a hunger for holiness.

Though I believe that all of the above is true, I still find myself asking God if He could come up with another plan. I wonder why He couldn't lead us to holiness by making our lives more comfortable. If He lavished all the blessings of heaven upon us, wouldn't that make us more grateful and devoted to Him, resulting in a holy life? It seems logical to me. Unfortunately, sin defies all rules of logic. The first man and woman enjoyed the best that God had to offer. Everything they wanted was as close as the nearest tree. They didn't have any problems at work to worry about or any Joneses to try to keep up with. Yet in spite of all of this, they turned away from God and sinned

The history of mankind, especially biblical history, shows the same pattern emerging time after time. In times of prosperity our natural human tendency is to forget God and to place our trust in what He has given us. We substitute our toys for God. As a result we don't have any time left over for Him. What choice does God have but to take our toys away as a severe act of mercy so that we will turn back to Him? Temporary suffering is a small price to pay if it results in hearts that genuinely long to be holy because He is holy.

Travel Log:

*1. Let's go back to the quiz at the beginning of this chapter. It seems strange to see ourselves placed alongside Mount Sinai and the tabernacle, but that is where God's Word places us. We're holy, set apart, different from the rest of the world. No one could use the holy things of the Old Testament for common uses. If holiness is necessary for tents and clothes, it is even more necessary for you and me. How are you treating the tabernacle of the New Testament, your own body?*_____

_____

What does your lifestyle say about the Holy One who set you apart?

_____

_____

*2. Being holy means more than abstaining from sin. True holiness comes from being set apart to God for His purpose and His glory. What do you think God has set you apart to do? What specific things does He want you to do?*_____

_____

*If you have trouble answering this question, stop and look around you through the eyes of the Lord. Can you see it now? Do you hear anyone groaning as sin takes a toll upon him?*_____

_____

As God's purpose begins to come into focus, stop and ponder this question: What price am I willing to pay to pursue His purpose for my life? _____

_____

*3. Holiness isn't optional for those who want to travel the path of faith. When we accept Jesus as our Savior we are declared to be holy positionally before the Father. From that moment on God sets out to bring what is true of us in heaven down to earth and into our day-to-day life. Our part of the process is to allow God to put to death everything in our lives that does not conform to His holiness. What needs to be put to death in your life?*_____

_____

What obstacles keep you from becoming more and more like Him?

_____

_____

Don't pass too quickly over these questions. Stop and spend some time alone with God discussing them with Him. This destination is far too important to pass by.

Chapter Three

THE
STEEP ROAD
OF PRAYER

I struggle with prayer. I understand how important it is, and I've gone through various study courses designed to make me a prayer warrior. I've heard stories about Martin Luther spending three hours in prayer before starting the day. Lack of information is definitely not my problem. No, I wrestle with the *act* of prayer. My mind wanders as my thoughts begin hip-hopping across the events of the day so that soon I have no idea what I was just praying about. When I get up early to pray I often fall asleep and feel very guilty when I wake up. Not that I don't feel guilty enough about prayer. I wish that I spent more time on my knees in the prayer closet (I don't even have a prayer closet; I usually pray in my office). On those rare occasions that I do feel satisfied with my praying, I often coast the next several days without praying at all.

I wish I could be more like the legends of the faith who prayed without end. John Hyde was such a man. George Mueller lived by faith and prayer. I haven't given up on prayer. On the contrary, it's a vital part of my life. But it's not easy. I've always thought that praying would someday become automatic, as natural as breathing. It hasn't, and I don't think it ever will.

I say all this to assure you that I am just like you. Unless you are an exception to the rule, you probably approach the subject of prayer with the same enthusiasm that most kids have when facing a plate of boiled spinach. You know it is good for you, but . . . Prayer for most of us is a steep incline that presents a constant challenge. Almost all of us struggle with our prayer lives. Few people feel that they pray enough. Even the mention of the word makes our anxiety level rise. "Guilty" would be the number one answer on "Family Feud" to the question "How do you feel about prayer?"

TRUE PRAYER

Part of our struggle comes from our understanding of the act of praying. We're not sure what it is or what it is meant to do. The entire process is a mystery. In prayer a sovereign God joins hands with the crowning point of His creation to do things that defy the imagination. By it empires have been toppled, fire has fallen from heaven, life-threatening illness has been taken away, eternal destinies have changed. Prayer gives us comfort in the midst of grief and heartache, boldness when we are tempted to give up. It warms our hearts and assures us that everything will be all right. But what is prayer?

The answer seems so obvious that we overlook it. The dictionary I consulted defines prayer as a solemn request or thanksgiving to God. Solemn—for some reason that word seems out of place, even though it is exactly how most of us think about prayer. We see it as a serious religious exercise to be carried out in hushed tones and dimly lit rooms. It gives prayer a heavy, eerie, and mystical quality, with key words and phrases that must be used to preserve its sanctity. High churches don't have a lock on this attitude. I see it everywhere, even among my fellow Southern Baptists. I've listened to friends who normally talk like Oklahoma rednecks suddenly begin speaking in a strange tongue, King James–style Elizabethian English to be exact, when they began to pray. "Thou who dost moveth in Thy providential ways, leadeth, guideth, and directeth Thou us." No doubt about it, solemn is the only word that can be used to describe this kind of praying.

The question I ask myself is whether or not this is what God has in mind when He talks about prayer. First Thessalonians tells us to pray without ceasing. I can't imagine being solemn without ceasing or talking like a Shakespearean actor without ceasing. No wonder we feel so guilty about prayer. We've separated it from real life in a way God never intended, and in the process we've lost our ability to pray. Those who can use the biggest, most mystical terms are lifted up as model prayers while the rest of us feel guilty. Enough is enough.

Perhaps no one has opened my eyes to the true nature of prayer like Charles Swindoll in his book, *Strengthening Your Grip*. Listen to how he describes it.

> Prayer was never intended to make us feel guilty. It was never intended to be a verbal marathon for only the initiated . . . no secret-code talk for the clergy or public display of piety. None of that. Real prayer—the kind Jesus mentioned and modeled—is realistic, spontaneous, down-to-earth communication with the living Lord that results in a relief of personal anxiety and a calm assurance that our God is in full control of our circumstances.[1]

My youngest daughter taught me how to pray like this. At the age of three she still had trouble with regular English, much less trying to imitate the sounds of a King James Bible. She had no idea what solemn meant. A three-year-old's understanding of who God is and what He is like is very limited. But she understood the essentials: God is God and He loves her. Moreover, she knew that when she talked to Him He heard her. She started every prayer with the same phrase, *Thank You*. Whether thanking God for the cottage cheese or asking God to give her aunt a baby, she always started by thanking Him.

I can't help but think that this is exactly what Paul had in mind when he said, "Do not be anxious about anything, but in everything, by prayer and petition, with thanksgiving, present your requests to God" (Philippians 4:6). The result of this kind of praying is that the "peace of God, which transcends all understanding, will guard your hearts and your minds in Christ Jesus" (Philippians 4:7). The whole idea of prayer is to take my burdens, worries, hopes, fears, joys, and sadness and turn it over to God:

adoring Him with a thankful heart that knows that He is in control of everything. He isn't impressed by eloquence. Three-year-olds understand this principle. They know that they can do nothing, but God can do anything and everything. Their confidence shows in the way they pray. We as adults need to become more like little children so that our praying can begin producing peace rather than anxiety.

Expectations in Prayer

As we begin praying, all of us have very definite, though perhaps unspoken, expectations of what will take place. Simply put, we expect God to do something, to do it quickly, and to do it as closely as possible to the manner we have prescribed to Him. No one ever puts these expectations into words, but they lie below the surface in the requests that we make of God. These are the underlying principles of the way my children make requests of me. Every time they ask for something they fully expect me to take action; otherwise, they would keep quiet or do it themselves. Whether it's to read them a book or get them something to eat or drink, they always expect some kind of results. "No" is a difficult concept for a child to grasp.

In prayer we also expect our heavenly Father to do something. That's why we go to all the trouble to ask. We may close every request with the pious phrase, "If it be Thy will," but deep down we fully expect God to take action on the issue we have brought to His attention, whether it be the salvation of a child or help making ends meet this month.

Children also expect results to come quickly. When they ask for something they expect it right away. They have no concept of time. According to their body clock a minute lasts exactly 3.5 seconds. That's how long they usually wait to ask again for a chocolate chip cookie when told the first time, "In a minute." They want action and they want it now.

Just as a child whose entire lifetime is five years has no concept of time in comparison to an adult, we who are temporal struggle with understanding time from God's perspective. We want action and we want it now. Even though we read Isaiah's exhortation to wait upon the Lord, we don't expect the waiting period to be very long. A week we can handle, a month starts stretching matters, a year is unbearable, beyond that is unthinkable.

When we pray, we not only want God to do something quickly, we also expect Him to do it according to the plan we have outlined to Him. I know that none of us would be so brash as to actually say this verbally, but the expectation is there deep within us. "Your will be done, O Lord, and here's how I would like it done," would be a good paraphrase of many of the prayers I have heard come out of my own mouth. Usually I find a way to cloak this desire with theologically correct phrases. But the bottom line is still the same: I have a plan and I want God to follow it. It's not that I think I can do a better job than God. Rather, I truly believe that I have a grasp on the situation and on what needs to be done to solve it. What other solution could there possibly be? This *must* be God's will.

Our Plans and God's Plan

The disciples thought they understood Jesus' method of operation after walking around Galilee and Judea with Him for three years. Therefore, when they asked if they should call down fire from the sky to destroy the Samaritan village that refused to allow them entry, they didn't think it was an odd request. Jesus was the ultimate prophet, so what would be more natural than to repeat one of Elijah's miracles, only on a grander scale? Many of our requests seem just as ridiculous with the passing of time. Even so, the basic expectation remains as we ask God to act according to the plan we give Him.

God usually surprises us and digresses from our plan. Though prayer is basically a child of God talking to his or her heavenly Father, there are times when the line seems to be disconnected or no longer in service. Many times our prayers are not answered. We ask God to act and He does not. We expect Him to go to work immediately, and we are told to wait. Though our plan seems flawless in our own eyes, God sets out doing something completely different, many times doing the very thing we had asked Him not to do. Is anyone home? Is He listening?

Now wait a minute, you say. Isn't the Bible filled with prayer promises? Didn't Jesus tell us that if two of us agree on something here on earth and pray, it would be done? How about the assurance 1 John 5 gives that if we ask anything according to His will He hears us and we have what we asked of Him? Aren't these promises still in the Bible?

The simple fact of the matter is that if God is listening to all our prayers, His answer is no more frequently than it is yes. I was asked recently by a woman whose husband had abandoned her why God hadn't saved this man. She had prayed earnestly for his salvation for years, as had her children. Rather than repent, he turned to a more and more decadent lifestyle until he couldn't stand living with her anymore. Her silent testimony and faithfulness to the Lord were like a twenty-four-hour sermon constantly confronting him with his sin. "Where was God in the midst of this? Why didn't He answer my prayers?" she asked me. I stumbled to find an answer.

The expectations we have as we pray are disappointed more often than they are satisfied. This was also true for many characters in the Bible. The most famous incident was Paul and his thorn in the flesh. Three times he prayed that God would remove it, and each time the answer came back the same: no. He fully expected God to do something, to give him relief from this constant source of frustration and pain. No doubt, he wanted God to do this as quickly as possible. The best way Paul could see to bring about relief was to remove the thorn. What could be simpler? The answer was still the same; the thorn stayed.

Silence from Heaven

Job would have welcomed an answer like Paul received. Any answer was better than the unbearable silence from heaven. As if the pain he was forced to endure were not enough, everything around him said that God had completely abandoned him. "Though I cry, 'I've been wronged!' I get no response; though I call for help, there is no justice" (19:7). "If only I knew where to find him; if only I could go to his dwelling!" (23:3). But for Job, God was nowhere to be found. The fellowship he had always enjoyed was now broken. No wonder he said, "What I feared has come upon me; what I dreaded has happened to me" (3:25). It wasn't the loss of his worldly wealth he feared. He had responded to that by saying, "Shall we accept good from God, and not trouble?" (2:10). But as day after day went by and his prayers were unheard and unanswered, his physical anguish gave way to a greater anguish in his soul.

Where is God while this is happening? Doesn't He hear? Why doesn't He answer? Have His promises failed, or is mankind so sinful that the promises are no longer valid? Have we misunderstood the promises that seemed so clear? The formula isn't working. We can either wrestle with these questions or put our heads in the sand and pretend it's not a problem. What do we do when God disappoints us in the arena of prayer?

The place to begin looking for answers is our basic understanding of what prayer is and what our expectations are when we pray. Remember Swindoll's definition of prayer as "realistic, spontaneous, down-to-earth communication with the living Lord that results in a relief of personal anxiety and a calm assurance that our God is in full control of our circumstances." So often this isn't the way we approach prayer. We see it as a magic formula that, hocus-pocus and amen, makes all our problems disappear. All you need to do is say the right words, claim the right prayer promises, and God is obligated to take care of the rest.

If God were an impersonal force floating about in the universe the formula might work. We could tap into His power anytime the mood struck us. He would be at our beck and call to go and do our bidding. God would have no choice but to do what we wanted if we used the right phrases and followed the right steps. The recipe would have to work. Aladdin never had it so good. I've sat through many prayer meetings where this seemed to be the god we were talking to.

But prayer is not a formula. It is a conversation between a child and a heavenly Father. The underlying purpose behind prayer is not results, but fellowship. In prayer I draw into the presence of the Sovereign Lord of the universe, the Creator of heaven and earth, the King over everything that is, was, and ever will be. Once there, I find that He is also my Father whose love knows no bounds and is not tainted by selfishness or sin.

Of course prayer changes things—the first thing it changes is me. Yet I must recognize that requests for myself and others are exactly that—requests, not demands. When I march into His presence with a shopping list and plop down on His lap as though He were wearing a red suit and beard at the shopping mall, I cannot help but be disappointed by the end result. But when I throw the list aside and pour out my heart to Him, He carries me through those disappointments. He also gives the calm assurance that He is aware of my situation and He is already at work doing what must be done.

Even so, there are times when God says no to the requests that we make. It's not that He hasn't heard or doesn't answer. The answer is loud and clear: No. I like yes a lot more. I've never cared much for the word *no*. Neither do my children. It's amazing the transformation this two-letter word can cause in their attitude and appearance. My three girls will come bouncing into the living room, full of giggles and smiles, their eyes sparkling (they know how to melt their old dad's heart). "Can we have something to eat? We're starving." (Children are never hungry or thirsty. They're always starving and about to die of thirst!) "No," I reply, sounding as cold and heartless to them as the worst of all the Iron Curtain dictators. The next words out of their mouths are always the same, "But why?" "Because you just had lunch fifteen minutes ago." While this sounds reasonable to me, it is absolutely ridiculous to a child suffering from the effects of being deprived of food for fifteen minutes. The next word is always the same, "Pleeeeaaaasssseeee." "No, maybe later." With that the same three angelic creatures who seemed to float into the room two minutes earlier now stalk out as if they were about to attend the funeral of their goldfish. That two-lettered horror has struck again.

Every parent has lived through a similar situation. There are times that we must say no to a child's requests. Children rarely think past the desires of the present to see their long-term effects. Parents must do that for them. It's our job, not to rob our children of all the fun and excitement of life, but to give them proper guidance. The worst thing anyone can do for children is to give them everything they want. Rather, we strive to give them what they need and withhold what they don't.

God, being the perfect Father, does the same thing in our lives. Because He loves us, He patiently ignores those requests that seem perfectly reasonable to us but will result in long-term problems. He does what is best, not what we want.

Waiting on God

Other times the answer isn't No but Not now. "When?" we always ask in reply.

"Just wait," the Lord tells us.

"OK, I've waited, now when?"

We sound a lot like the original disciples who were constantly asking Jesus when He was going to set up His kingdom. In fact, it was the very last question they asked Him before He ascended into heaven. "Lord, are You at this time going to restore the kingdom to Israel?" A loose paraphrase of Jesus' response is, "For the umpteenth time, no and no, I'm not going to tell you when. Just wait and do what I have left you here to do."

The Lord is constantly telling us the same thing. We expect Him to act according to our timetable, but He never does. Yet, unbelievably, He's never late; He never misses a deadline. It seemed like He was late when Lazarus died. "If You'd only been here he wouldn't have died. Oh, Jesus, You're too late." He may have been too late to heal Lazarus from the fatal disease that had taken his life, but He was right on time to raise him from the dead. That had been the plan all along.

Not only do we wrestle with understanding God's timing, but we often find God deviating from the script we've given Him. Lazarus is the classic example. Jesus is Lord, and therefore He works according to His master plan. While we have a part in that plan as God accomplishes much of His work through us and in response to our prayers, we don't dictate policy to God. Our prayer is always to be, "not my will but Yours be done."

Most of the time God answers prayer in ways we never anticipate. Paul experienced this when he prayed for the removal of his thorn in the flesh. Earlier we looked at how God said no to Paul's request, but that's not the end of the story. Rather than do what Paul asked, the Lord said, "My grace is sufficient for you, for my power is made perfect in weakness." Paul responded with renewed confidence, "Therefore I will boast all the more gladly about my weaknesses, so that Christ's power may rest on me. That is why, for Christ's sake, I delight in weaknesses, in insults, in hardships, in persecutions, in difficulties. For when I am weak, then I am strong" (2 Corinthians 12:9–10).

Paul was seeking a demonstration of God's power for the moment in the removal of that which was a hardship. God taught Paul that His power could rest on him permanently, even in the midst of the harshest adversity. The great missionary did not get what he asked for—he received much, much more.

Times come when we can say with all certainty that God didn't make things turn out the way that we wanted, and what we received in return couldn't be God's will. He doesn't want homes to disintegrate or rebellious children to reject their parents and run away from home. How could He possibly want His children to suffer through prolonged illness? Yet these are sometimes "results" of our most earnest, heartfelt praying. It is an insult to our intelligence to say that God's alternative plan was to bring into reality a worst-case scenario as these prayers go unanswered.

THE LESSONS OF UNANSWERED PRAYER

What is God trying to teach us when we face the dilemma of unanswered prayer? First and foremost, He is training us to trust Him even when we don't understand what is happening. Faith is not believing *for* something, it is believing *in* Someone. Faith tied to results isn't faith at all and leads only to frustration and disappointment. But faith that trusts the God who loves us is able to weather disappointments and come out safe on the other side. The former is nothing more than a sanctified consumer mentality. The latter is the essence of biblical faith that leads to a personal relationship with the living Lord.

Yes, there are times that prayer seems to go unanswered in this journey of faith. But God remains faithful. With the passage of time we often see that God is powerful and sovereign enough to take the worst of nightmares and use them for His glory. In the end we, like Paul, will be able to rejoice in our adversities, for when we are weak, He is strong.

NOTE

1. Charles Swindoll, *Strengthening Your Grip: Essentials in an Aimless World* (Waco, Tex.: Word, 1982), 157.

Travel Log:

1. This chapter doesn't address how to pray, but rather what to expect as we pray. That's why prayer is a way to walk the paths along the journey, rather than a destination. I've been honest with you, I struggle with prayer. Now it's your turn. How is your prayer life? _____

Is it a formal, religious exercise or free and open communication with God? _____

Are you satisfied with the amount of time you spend praying? _____ *If you are, should you be? If you are not, what keeps you from praying more?* _____

When is the act of prayer most natural? _____ *When is it most difficult?* _____

2. A recurring theme in this chapter addresses our expectations when we pray. This takes us back to the first question at the close of the first chapter. When we set out on the adventure of faith we expect God to do certain things. We find the clearest picture of these expectations in our prayer life. Look back on the things you've asked God about over the past week. What do they tell you about your expectations? _____

Think about more than simply the requests you've made of God. Consider the timetable you would like Him to work under. Does it seem reasonable? How close does it come to God's schedule? _____

_____

3. Prayer is an exercise with results. As we go through this uncommon adventure, times will come when God will give us what we ask as well as times when His answer will be no. Think about the times God has granted your requests. How often has the answer come quickly? _____ *When it was delayed, what did you do?* _____ *Has He ever said yes and later you wished the answer had been no?* _____

*Very often God's answer is no. We don't like hearing that word, especially from God. Think about some specific requests He has refused to give you. Why do you think His answer was no?*_____

How would your life be different if He had granted your requests?

_____

_____

Sometimes we never understand His reason for turning us down. In those moments He asks us to trust Him. You may be struggling right now to do this very thing. Spend some time talking to Him about it. You may not find any answers, but you will find He still loves you and is working in your life. Trust Him.

Chapter Four

SOME UNUSUAL
TRAVELING
COMPANIONS

The trails within Sequoia National Forest are dec-
orated with signs that are less than comforting
to the novice outdoorsman. In bold letters they proclaim:
WARNING, BEAR COUNTRY! Below these words are instructions of how one can minimize the possibility of having a personal, face-to-face encounter with a bear.

I take these signs very, very seriously. Having grown up in a part
of the world where bears were only found on television, I have
some preconceived ideas of what they are like. Most of them are a
sort of hairy, ten-foot tall, great white shark on legs. Their favorite
dish is camper wrapped in flannel, as in sleeping bag lining.

Because I know how ferocious bears are, I make my family
take every precaution possible to minimize the chance of a bear
encounter. Every scrap of food is either burned or locked away in
airtight containers. My three girls then search every square inch
of the campsite for any crumbs large enough to entice a bear to
come calling during the night. Finally, as a last act before bed-
time, I take the clothes we have worn through the day—clothes

that may harbor a scent of food—and lock them away as well.

Funny thing. I have only seen one bear while hiking through the forest. He didn't look at all like the ferocious creature Clint Walker battled in *Night of the Grizzly*. In fact, this bear took one look at us, mumbled something to himself like, "There goes the neighborhood," and trotted off into the woods. Even so, I still do everything possible to protect myself from the grizzlies I fear are lurking behind every tree.

Though bears are in short supply on most camping trips, flies, gnats, and other assorted insects are always plentiful. From ants on the picnic table to the constant buzzing of one lone mosquito in the tent at night, every hiking trip I have taken has been filled with bugs. The two official hand motions of campers are the slap and the scratch. Yet, in spite of all this, the bug repellent is usually forgotten until the middle of the night when it is needed the most. Then I remember that it's under the sink at home.

Bears seldom ruin trips through the forest. Insects rarely leave them alone. The threat of bears and the presence of bugs are constants of every camper's experience in the Sequoia National Forest. In the same manner, trials are a constant companion on the journey of faith. Most of us fear the great, life-shattering trials and take every precaution against them. Other trials are small and hardly given a thought until they come like gnats in a swarm. In addition, there are other tests of a believer's faith that seem to go on forever. Though they seem small at the outset, by their persistence their apparent size and strength increases.

No one is immune from adversity. Faith is not a magic wand that causes troubles to disappear. Nor are trials fair in their selection process. Many people are born into the midst of trials greater than anyone should have to endure. Others have such tests cast upon them simply because of their newfound faith in Christ. Whatever adversity's cause, however long its duration, few steps are taken on this journey without its unwelcome company. Some of the trials we face are devastating, faith-testing events. Others are merely pesky. Let's look at a few.

GNATS

The third plague upon Egypt in the book of Exodus was the smallest of the ten. It consisted of small, annoying insects: gnats.

A gnat is not usually considered the kind of animal that can topple an empire. A rolled-up newspaper and swift reflexes are all you need to get rid of one. Yet it was this third plague that prompted Pharaoh's advisers to cry out, "This is the finger of God." Their fear came not from the size of the insect but from its numbers. The gnats were as numerous as the dust of the earth.

Many of the trials that accompany us on a daily basis are like the gnats in Egypt. When looked at individually they hardly call for a second look. They appear small and insignificant. Yet small trials rarely travel alone. Like gnats, they come in swarms.

Persistent Buzzing

A distinctive buzz announces the gnats' arrival. It takes the form of phrases like . . .

> "Mr. Tabb, this is the school. Your daughter fell and . . ."
> "Is this your mangy, garbage-eating dog? . . ."
> "Oops."
> "Honey, have you seen the superglue?"
> "Moooommmm, does grape juice stain?"
> "Has there always been a dent on this side of the car?"
> "The boss would like to see you. By the way, did you remember that the Wilson account was supposed to be renewed last month?"
> "You want it when?"

You get the picture. We've all had the calm of the day broken with sound bites like these as the gnats travel over from Egypt and invade our lives. What's odd is how they travel in swarms. The damage they create individually is never great. It's their cumulative effect that makes our lives miserable.

Days will go by when life is smooth and trouble-free. Then, suddenly, everything falls apart at the same time.

Human Responses to Gnat Trials

I play a game that rolls all these elements into one fun-packed four-hour period. It is innocently referred to as golf. The object of the game is simple enough: knock a ball in a hole with a stick. What could be easier? Unfortunately, the ball and the hole are five hundred yards apart and the chasm between them is filled with sand, water, tall grass, and ball-eating trees. Somehow the game is supposed to help me relax. How can I relax with this constant buzzing?

Golf has a way of bringing out the worst in people. I have played with Christian friends who have thrown clubs into the air and into trees out of frustration. Others go from talking about how wonderful the Lord is on the first tee to mumbling assorted profanities by the eighteenth. This is often our first reaction to the continuous onslaught of the gnats: anger. To say we lose our joy is an understatement. Gnat trials have a way of transforming one from a mild-mannered Christian husband and father into nitroglycerin, liable to explode with the slightest provocation.

These trials baffle us and take away our pride. They seem so small that we are sure we can handle them in our own strength. No one ever prays that God would kill a bug. We feel certain that we can smash them. But we cannot. They remind us of our limitations and our need to rely on the One who is greater than us in every aspect of life.

Our second reaction is to try to escape to the greener grass that must exist somewhere in this world. When gnats invade our workplace we begin to long for the escape the weekend promises. When I was attending Bible college I dreamed of the free and easy road that seemed to exist in the wonderful, post-graduation world. But there are gnats in every paradise we seek.

At times I find myself wondering why God doesn't create a giant can of Raid and kill all the gnats that buzz into my life. Unfortunately, gnats are permanent this side of eternity. Days when everything seems to go wrong have a very important purpose in our lives. They are some of the most accurate barometers of the validity of our faith. By constantly scratching at the surface of our lives they reveal what is really inside us. If God did remove them the single greatest opportunity we have to outwardly demonstrate Christ with our lives would be taken away. The world is watching to see if what we say we believe is real. Our reactions, not our actions, are the transmitters upon which this information is broadcast.

GOPHERS

Several years ago I uprooted my young family and moved

them to the foothills of the Sierra Nevada Mountains in California. At that time I did not realize that the land upon which we would live is made of solid rock. Apart from a thin layer of topsoil, the dirt is made up of something we affectionately refer to as decomposed granite, which is interspersed with real granite. During the dry summer months, when the average rainfall is two reruns of "Singing in the Rain," it is virtually impossible to dig a hole deeper than one inch. The ground stubbornly refuses to yield to a shovel.

Thus, I was shocked to discover gopher mounds throughout my yard. Somehow this cousin of the rat was able to dig its way through solid rock and make a mess of my lawn. Part of my backyard looked like a war zone. I tried everything short of firepower to get rid of him. Nothing worked. One day I even shoved a water hose down the gopher hole in an attempt to drown the pest. The next day he left his distinctive calling card as if to say, "Thanks for the bath."

Some of the trials that hitch a ride with us are like gophers. They stubbornly refuse to go away despite all our best efforts to get rid of them. Here I am not referring to the major, lingering trials that devastate our lives. We will examine those later. Gopher trials are the ones that are frustrating. While they don't destroy our lives, they are able to make life miserable.

Major appliances are a favorite nesting place of gopher trials. I recently completed twelve months of warfare with one that took up residence inside our automatic ice-maker. One day the water tube leading into the ice-maker was plugged with ice, a simple problem to fix. So I fixed it. The next day the ice had returned, and the next and the next and the next. I realized that I had a bigger problem somewhere. Thus, I disassembled every part of the ice-maker from top to bottom. I cleaned and finagled and followed all the advice I was given over the toll-free repair hot line. Nothing worked. Finally, I waved the white flag, giving the machine to the gopher as a gift. Then, without warning, it began making ice again. The problem disappeared, and I have no idea why.

Some physical ailments fall into the gopher category, especially allergies. For all my adult life I've lived with itchy, watery eyes, a runny nose, constant sneezing, and doing without ice cream (I'm allergic to milk, among other things). Though rarely life-threatening, allergies take away the incentive to wake up in the morning. All the remedies advertised have a minimal effect when the peak ragweed season strikes. Frustrating is an understatement in describing the trial allergies become.

Trying Patience

Sometimes human beings mutate into gophers. We all have one special someone who fits this description, some person who tries our patience just by breathing. Be it by their personalities, their laughs, or their general outlook on life, the people God places in our lives test our Christianity on a daily basis. Some commentators believe that Paul was speaking of just such a person when he told of the thorn in his flesh in 2 Corinthians 12. He called his thorn a "messenger of Satan" sent to torment him. The term "messenger" is used in every other New Testament occurrence to refer to a literal being, either human, angelic, or demonic. Therefore, it is logical to assume that Paul uses the term here to refer to someone who continually tried his patience and tormented him by his presence.

Persistence

Whoever this person may have been, he is a classic example of persistent, frustrating trials. This thorn in the flesh, this messenger of Satan, simply would not go away. Three times Paul prayed that God would do something to deliver him. No doubt his intensity increased with each request. If he was like me, all formality was gone when he prayed the third time. His prayer was closer to the desperate cry of a drowning man than a religious exercise. Yet each time God's answer was the same: No.

Persistence is the most trying aspect of gopher trials. Once the gophers have us in their sights, they refuse to relinquish their attack. What starts as little more than an annoyance soon grows into a enormous frustration. Like water upon a rock they wear us down, robbing us of our joy, making life miserable. They take us to our breaking point, where we simply can't endure anything more. If this were warfare, the gophers would be winning.

How can something like this defeat us? How can something that appears to be well within our ability to overcome take us to the brink of surrender? I believe there are two reasons. First, we underestimate the size of the adversary. A single gopher mound in a yard doesn't mean that only one gopher has invaded. So too, below what appears on the surface to be a rather small and simple test of our faith may lurk a much greater problem.

In Our Own Strength

This leads us to the second reason that gopher trials defeat us. While underestimating their size we overestimate our strength. We tell ourselves that we can handle it. Prayer is not our line of first defense. Rather than depending upon God, we depend upon our own ability. Soon we discover that we are overwhelmed. Yet this can lead to embarrassment and hinder our cries for help. We don't want to admit defeat; we're embarrassed that something so small could devastate us so.

All this leads us to God's purpose in allowing such trials into our lives. God's answer to Paul when he asked for deliverance from his thorn in the flesh wasn't a simple no. Second Corinthians 12:9 records the Lord's timeless answer to Paul and to all of us who are weary from wrestling gophers, "My grace is sufficient for you, for my power is made perfect in weakness." God uses trying people and persistent difficulties to expose our own weaknesses that we might learn to depend upon the power of His grace. Once we learn this lesson we will be able to say with Paul, "Therefore I will boast all the more gladly about my weaknesses, so that Christ's power may rest on me. That is why, for Christ's sake, I delight in weaknesses, in insults, in hardships, in persecutions, in difficulties. For when I am weak, then I am strong" (2 Corinthians 12:9b–10).

GRIZZLY BEARS

Most of us live in fear that something terrible and traumatic will sweep down upon us and change our lives forever. Whereas gnat-like trials are annoying and gopher trials are frustrating, grizzly bear trials are totally devastating. Their names read like a who's who of disaster. Cancer, bankruptcy, divorce, a runaway child—all the things we fear the most.

Thus, we take every step possible to protect ourselves from their onslaught. Millions of dollars each year are spent on insurance policies, security systems, high-fiber cereals, and exercise equipment. Like campers locking their food away in airtight containers, prudence demands that we take these steps to minimize the chances of coming face to face with catastrophe.

The Devastation of a Grizzly Attack

But there are times that everything we do to protect ourselves isn't enough. Job lived through our worst nightmare when his life was rocked one fateful day. He too was a man of caution, offering sacrifices for sins that his children *might* have committed. Moreover, he was a good and holy man. God Himself said, "There is no one on earth like him; he is blameless and upright, a man who fears God and shuns evil" (Job 1:8). Yet none of this protected Job from the devastation that awaited him.

When calamity struck Job, it struck with a vengeance. In one day he suffered the loss of all of his flocks, herds, and camels, the measure of wealth in the ancient Near East. If this had been the totality of his suffering he might have survived intact. But an even greater pain struck Job. All ten of his children died when the house in which they were holding a feast collapsed. Suddenly this great man, a man who was admired by all those around him, was left penniless and grief-stricken. But more was on the way. A terrible skin disease struck Job, covering him from head to toe with sores. The sight of him was so horrible that his friends did not recognize him when they came to comfort him.

In a very brief period of time Job encountered most of the bears we fear the most. Financial ruin, the death of children, and sickness were all thrust upon this one man, leaving him helpless to do anything about his situation. Sometimes we read about Job's reaction to all of this and wonder who the hero of the story really is. He utters words that show the depth of his pain. Listen to a sample:

> What I feared has come upon me; what I dreaded has happened to me. I have no peace, no quietness; I have no rest, but only turmoil. (Job 3:25–26)

> If only my anguish could be weighed and all my misery be placed on the scales! It would surely outweigh the sand of the seas. (Job 6:2–3)

> I loathe my very life; therefore I will give free rein to my complaint and speak out in the bitterness of my soul. I will say to God: Do not condemn me, but tell me what charges you have against me. (Job 10:1–2)

We don't expect words like this from a saint. They sound more like the cry of one whose soul has been crushed than one who is rejoicing in adversity. He simply asks the same question each one of us asks when disaster strikes, "Why, God? Why did this happen to me?" Job was very human and his words reflect that fact. Perhaps the most difficult part of the trials he endured was the isolation he felt from God. His prayers seemed to bounce off the ceiling and fall to the floor unheard and unanswered.

The Helplessness of a Grizzly Attack

Mercifully, most of us will not experience the depth of despair Job had to endure. Yet at the same time, we have no guarantees that disaster will spare us from its uninvited presence. We all know people—perhaps you are one of them—who have had to endure bitter, bitter trials. No one can really understand the pain that descends upon the soul in that hour. No one can relate to the helplessness such sufferers feel. Hearing that God is in control and that He'll make everything work out for good rings hollow when one is dealing with life-shattering grief. It's impossible to keep wearing a smile when the only prayer a person can muster is "Oh, God, why?"

These days come. Our greatest nightmares do come true. Trials as big and ferocious as grizzly bears attack believers as well as unbelievers. Yet there is one wonderful assurance we have as we travel with Jesus Christ. No matter how terrible or devastating the storm may be, we never go through it alone. Before He ascended into heaven, Jesus made us a promise that He would never leave or forsake us. Thus, not only will He be with us when trials strike, He will not abandon us in the middle of them. Knowing this, we are able to endure any trial, no matter how ferocious the bear may be.

Gnats, gophers, and grizzly bears are out there waiting for us as we walk with Christ. Clinging to His hand by faith doesn't insulate us from any of them. The rain falls on the just and the unjust, and the flood waters they spawn can damage the property of the righteous as well as the unrighteous. We will face trials. Our faith will be tested on a daily basis, for God never promised us a trouble-free life. Knowing this, we can prepare ourselves for the hardships that lie ahead on the path of faith.

Travel Log:

*1. Gnats have a way of flying over from Egypt and finding us as we follow the Lord down the path of faith. No one is immune to the incessant buzzing. What kind of buzzing insects have you encountered this week?*_____

_____

What did you do to get rid of them? _____

_____

*The statement was made earlier in the chapter that gnats are "barometers of the validity of our faith. By constantly scratching at the surface of our lives they reveal what is really inside us." What have the gnats in your life revealed about you? Have they confirmed or damaged your testimony?*_____

_____

*2. God can use everything, even gophers. He assured Paul that his thorn in the flesh would reveal his weaknesses so that he would learn to rely on the power of God. What persistent, gopherlike trials are you battling?*_____

_____

*The list includes physical ailments, problems on the job, or a personality conflict. What weaknesses in you have these trials revealed?*___

_____

*Now let's get very transparent before God. How have you responded to the gophers in your life? Have they drawn you closer to the Lord by forcing you to rely on His strength, or have they left you tired and frustrated?*_____

*Here is a simple test to see how you are doing in your wrestling match with the rodents: Can you rejoice in your weakness and in the trial, or are you still begging God to take it away?*_____

---

*3. Calling trials gnats, gophers, and grizzly bears may seem humorous, but there is nothing funny about the latter when they strike us personally. Isolation covers us like a fog. It seems that no one can truly relate to what we are going through. I cannot imagine the depth of despair Job endured. Perhaps you have shared some of his experiences. Looking back, how did God make Himself known to you as you walked through the fire?*_____

---

*Which promises from His Word came alive like never before?*_____

---

*Were there friends who came and shared your grief?*_____

*What did you learn through the storm that you can share with others who are now going through a similar trial?*_____

It may well be that you can't answer these questions because the pain is still too great and God seems terribly far away. Please remember, the Lord Himself knows how you feel. He too went through the agony of the death of one He loves when His Son died upon a cross. While no one else may understand how you feel right now, He does. And you can talk to Him about it. Please, pour out your heart to Him. He's not far away; He's close to your side, waiting to hear from you.

Chapter Five

REMADE
ALONG
THE WAY

$\mathcal{I}$ have a friend with an amazing talent. He has the ability to take a large piece of stone and remake it into any shape he desires. He is the first sculptor I've ever met. My curiosity finally got the best of me and I had to ask him how he did it. How could he take a chunk of rock and in the course of a few months turn it into a piece of art? The answer is simple enough: He chips away everything that doesn't look like the final product he hopes to create.

You and I have a lot in common with the rocks my friend works with. The Bible says that we come to Christ as living stones. God looks at us, with all our rough edges and sharp cracks, and sees a masterpiece modeled after His Son Jesus Christ. Throughout the rest of our lives He sets out to make this masterpiece a reality. Slowly He chips away everything in us that doesn't look like Christ until we are conformed to His image in every way. God doesn't confine this work to a select few. All of us who set out on a pilgrimage with Christ will find God diligently working to bring us to maturity.

The idea of a sculptor chipping away at a stone helps us to understand the process God takes us through to bring us to spiritual maturity. James describes it this way, "Consider it pure joy, my brothers, whenever you face trials of many kinds, because you know that the testing of your faith develops perseverance. Perseverance must finish its work so that you may be mature and complete, not lacking anything" (James 1:2–4). Trials are the hammer and chisel God uses to reshape us in the image of His Son. James isn't the only biblical writer to propose that God's preferred *modus operandi* for perfecting His children is adversity. The Lord Himself in the analogy of the vine and the branches stated that every branch that is fruitful is pruned so that it will bear more fruit. While the pruning process may be painful, it is necessary for the branches to reach their full potential. Paul describes the process in Romans 5:

> Not only so, but we also rejoice in our sufferings, because we know that suffering produces perseverance; perseverance, character; and character, hope. And hope does not disappoint us, because God has poured out his love into our hearts by the Holy Spirit, whom he has given us. (vv. 3–5)

The process Paul describes goes through three steps. The first step is perseverance. The early church faced the temptation to give up on a daily basis. Between the peer pressure of living in a decadent society to the outright hostility of the first-century world to the gospel, being a Christian was a difficult path to choose. We usually think of perseverance in terms of Calvin's five points, a purely theological exercise. It was much more to those who received Paul's letters. His words gave them the encouragement they needed to hold fast to Jesus for another day.

PERSEVERANCE UNDER GOD'S TOOLS

The farther we go down the path of faith, the more difficult the journey becomes. In the early stages, we're full of the enthusiasm and excitement that mark a new Christian. Traveling with the Lord is the greatest experience we could ever imagine. With time the steps get harder to take. The road stretches on forever, and unpleasant surprises spring at us at every bend. More often than most of us would like to admit we reach a point where we want to stop and forget the whole thing. The first stage of maturity is finding the perseverance to keep going, even when it's the last thing we want to do.

THE CHARACTER OF CHRISTLIKENESS

As perseverance develops, the character of Christ begins to emerge within us. Paul described this as the second step in the maturing process. But it is much more than a step: It is the centerpiece of what God wants to accomplish in our lives. The closer we grow to God the more we want to be like Him. Although we are helpless to produce Christlike character in our daily lives, God through His Holy Spirit is working to bring it about. Day in, day out, He patiently chips and polishes until we attain "to the whole measure of the fullness of Christ" (Ephesians 4:13).

God doesn't intend for this to be some sort of mystical ideal confined to religious circles. Jesus invaded the world of physical reality when He came to this earth. Thus, the image of Christ in us is real, and it changes the way we live our daily lives. It begins with a changed perspective on life. When God remakes us in the image of His Son, He opens our eyes to see the world as Jesus did. Satan offered Jesus all the kingdoms of this world, but our Lord cared only about the kingdom that was to come. In the same way, being remade in the image of Christ will take away our affection for this world and cause us to seek first "the kingdom of God and His righteousness."

Mature Passions

We'll also begin to share Jesus' devotion and passion. His only desire while walking on this earth was to do the will of His Father. Listen to His words, as recorded by John:

> I tell you the truth, the Son can do nothing by himself; he can do only what he sees his Father doing, because whatever the Father does the Son also does. . . . I seek not to please myself but him who sent me. (John 5:19, 30)

The mark of spiritual maturity is a burning desire to do the will of God. God's will for His Son was to seek and to save those who are lost. Before He ascended into heaven our Lord told His disciples that they were to finish the work He had started. Just as He came to preach the gospel, we too are to be actively involved in evangelism, telling the good news to all who will listen. Sometimes we associate a passion for witnessing with the euphoria of a new Christian, something that will wear off with time. But true maturity produces a greater passion for evangelism, not a slow cooling of the desire to see people saved.

Jesus also had a passion for God. He carved out chunks of time from His schedule to spend time alone with His Father. Mark's gospel records that He often went to a solitary place to pray. Before making major decisions, as when He chose the twelve disciples, He spent the night in prayer. He prepared for His greatest moment of agony and trial, His arrest and crucifixion, by talking intimately with His Father. As the Holy Spirit conforms us to the image of Christ, He will produce within us a similar burning desire to know God intimately and to spend time alone with Him.

Mature Love

Love characterized not only Jesus' relationship with the Father, but also all of His life. It drove Him to the cross to give His life as a sin offering for our forgiveness. Those of us who claim to be Christians—to be Christlike—will share His love. In fact, Jesus said love was to be the standard by which the validity of our faith is measured: "By this all men will know that you are my disciples, if you love one another" (John 13:35). By His example Jesus showed us that this love is to be sacrificial, a love that considers others to be more important than ourselves. If you've spent much time in the human race you've probably found that this kind of love is impossible on a human level. God knew this. That is why He has poured out His love into our hearts as Paul wrote about in Romans 5:5. What is impossible on our own becomes a reality as He reshapes us in the image of His Son.

Humility and Boldness

Christlike character also produces humility and boldness. The two almost appear to be mutually exclusive terms, but in Christ they come together. Philippians 2 describes the humiliation Jesus went through on our behalf in leaving heaven and taking on flesh. He demonstrated humility as He avoided the accolades of the crowds and associated with those the world had tagged as undesirable. Intermingled with humility was boldness. How else can you describe a man who stood up against the religious establishment of His day and demanded they repent? Reading the confrontations between Jesus and the Pharisees amazes me. Anyone else would have quietly left town. Not Jesus. He boldly stood and proclaimed, "The kingdom of God is near! Repent and believe the good news!"

Humility and boldness are two qualities in short supply as we near the end of the twentieth century. Few believers choose to take the lower places, to associate with the undesirable elements of our society. Perhaps this is most apparent in the brand of Christianity that comes into homes via television. Ornate sets and palatial sanctuaries come across as a plea for respect from the world and, as a result, they silence the church's prophetic voice. Real boldness is almost impossible to find. Studies show that fewer than 5 percent of confessing Christians ever witness of their faith. God's hammer and chisel still have a lot of work to do.

Servanthood

Of all the character qualities of Jesus, one stands above all the rest. To be like Christ is to become a servant. Jesus Himself declared that He didn't come to be served but to serve and to give His life as a ransom for many. In case there were any doubts about what He meant, He washed the disciples' feet. We'll devote an entire chapter later to the subject of becoming servants. At this point one thing needs to be very clear: If Jesus came to be a servant, and if God is reshaping us in the image of Jesus, it only stands to reason that God's plan is for us to give up our lives in service to others. To be like Christ, to be spiritually mature, is to be a servant.

HOPE

The final stage of the maturity process described in Romans 5 is hope. It seems odd to find hope as the final product of suffering. In our day we have come to equate adversity with losing hope, especially when the situation progresses from bad to worse.

The closing days of twentieth-century America testify to this. Our country has digressed into a nation of victims. Because of economic deprivation or racial tension or gender bias or dysfunctional families we have given up optimism for the future. Even the church has fallen prey to this. We focus on what's wrong with our world to the point that all hope is lost.

The mark of maturity in Christ is hope in the midst of suffering. This isn't a blind desire that the future will be brighter than today. Rather, it's the mark of God's love in our heart. We have hope in God, not in the world system. Paul goes on to say, "And hope does not disappoint us, because God has poured out his love into our hearts by the Holy Spirit, whom he has given us" (Romans 5:5). Maturity comes when we are able to cling to the love of God and know that He is with us no matter what our circumstances may be. This goes beyond enduring suffering for the sake of Christ to being able to rejoice in the midst of it.

TRAPS OF DEFEAT

No doubt those of us who claim to know Christ personally as our Lord and Savior would say that we want God to bring us to this destination; we want to be spiritually mature. At the moment of conversion God brings about a radical change of heart that makes us long to be like Him. At the same time we learn to hate the remnants of sin we find within ourselves. Unfortunately, we get used to being part of God's family, and our desire to be like Christ starts to cool. Like Paul's cry in Romans 7, we often find ourselves doing the very thing we hate. Conversely, the good that we desire to do is forgotten and left undone. This wrestling match is constantly going on deep within our hearts and minds. The moment we think we are victorious, defeat suddenly overwhelms us.

Too Easily Satisfied

Therefore, the task God faces of conforming each one of us to the image of His Son is no small chore. More often than not the greatest obstacle He faces is the very person He is working on. It's not only falling back into the old ways of life that causes a problem. A greater obstacle is our tendency to become satisfied very quickly with the level of progress we have achieved. Like the tribes of Reuben and Gad, we're eager to stop short of the Promised Land and settle for something less than God's best. We achieve a certain level of biblical understanding, perhaps from reading the Bible in its entirety, and we are satisfied. More than that, we become proud of how much we have come to know without realizing that our ignorance far outweighs our knowledge. Other parts of the Christian life are no different. In the battle against sin we gauge our progress by looking at the world around us rather than looking up at Christ. As long as we're a step or two above the crowd we're content. While the world is renting R-rated films we never go beyond PG-13, as though such a decision is a great sacrifice. We grow so comfortable with the progress that God has made in us that we assume the journey is over and now is the time to relax.

Solomon fell into this trap. In the early days of his reign he felt the full weight of his responsibility as shepherd over the nation of Israel, and he fell on his face before God. When God gave him his choice of any gift, Solomon could only think of one thing—wisdom. Gold and silver or all the riches on earth couldn't give him what he needed to survive as the successor to the throne of the "man after God's own heart." But as Solomon began to enjoy the prosperity and independence that God poured out upon the kingdom, his heart grew cold. The man who had sacrificed twenty-two thousand cattle and one hundred twenty thousand sheep and goats to the Lord when the temple was dedicated was found at the end of his life building altars to the gods of the Moabites and the Ammonites.

I believe this is one of the primary reasons that God has chosen to use adversity as a path to maturity. No one has stated this more masterfully than C. S. Lewis in *The Problem of Pain*:

> Now God, who has made us, knows what we are and that our happiness lies in Him. Yet we will not seek it in Him as long as He leaves us any other resort where it can plausibly be looked for. While what we call "our own life" remains agreeable we will not surrender it to Him. What then can God do in our interests but make "our own life" less agreeable to us, and take away the plausible sources of false happiness?[1]

As long as we can comfortably remain at any point along the spiritual pilgrimage, we will. Thus, God has to make us uncomfortable to move us along. Lewis goes on to describe this as an act of Divine Humility, where God is willing to accept our turning to Him when we have no other place to go.

I've seen this process take place many, many times as I have served God as a pastor. Without fail, every time a member of my church begins to grow in the Lord and the excitement that comes with growth begins to blossom, trials arrive. They are the entrance exams to the next level of maturity. The tests are multifaceted. Some arrive in the form of financial setbacks, others as conflicts with other Christians. Life becomes less agreeable, as a means of turning excitement into maturity.

Adversity and Bitterness

Making life less agreeable doesn't in and of itself make us mature. Often the reverse is true. As life becomes less sweet we become bitter. Adversity can just as easily result in anger toward God as it can prod us toward spiritual maturity. The parable of the sower teaches us that trials are used by God to separate those who have genuinely been converted from those who are merely attracted to the good stuff God offers. The key factor upon which the entire equation hinges is faith. It separates the plants that shrivel and die from those that produce a bumper crop.

There is more to the maturing process that adversity brings about than simply refocusing our attention upon God. Faith in the midst of suffering rejoices in the fact that there is victory through our Lord Jesus Christ. This victorious note is sounded throughout the New Testament. I love how Romans 8:35–37 puts this wonderful promise:

> *Who shall separate us from the love of Christ?*
> *Shall trouble or hardship or persecution or famine or*
> *nakedness or danger or sword? As it is written:*
> *"For your sake we face death all day long;*
> *we are considered as sheep to be slaughtered."*
> *No, in all these things we are more than conquerors*
> *through him who loved us.*

More than conquerors *in* all these things. The victory has nothing to do with the cessation of suffering. No, in the midst of the worst of circumstances we are victorious in Jesus Christ our Lord. The One who conquered sin and death for all time isn't about to surrender His children to defeat.

Thus, martyrs throughout the history of the church have been able to raise their hands in victory even as their lives are being taken away. Because of the victory we have in Christ a man like Horatio Spafford was able to say "It is well with my soul" even as his heart was broken with grief over the deaths of his children. And because of the victory I have in Christ, I am able to rejoice in the midst of any and all circumstances. By faith I know that the presence of trials in my life is a visible sign that God hasn't forgotten me and that He is hard at work making me more like Christ.

Maturity, then, comes through the testing of our faith, by pushing it to the limit and finding even there that God is faithful. No matter what may come, in Him we are victorious. Victory comes not by the elimination of pain but by God's faithfulness through the midst of suffering. In this way we can be, like our Lord, made perfect through suffering.

Wow! Stop and think about this concept for a while. Does it make your heart beat a little faster to think about how freeing this is? The world tries to escape pain, but God uses it to take us farther along the journey of faith. The road may be rough and rocky, but how wonderful the destination will be!

Tests of Strength

God has other ways to bring us to this place called maturity. Before trials come and test us, we are unable to see what our true weaknesses are. Like weak links in a chain, they are never discovered until our lives are placed under stress. Then, not only are they exposed, but we are desperate to have them fixed. The tests we took as children in school served this same purpose. Not only were they a tool for the teachers to see how much we knew, they also allowed them to see what we did not know. As a result, they could direct our attention to study harder in our weaker subjects.

God exposes our weaknesses through trials, not so that we can redouble our efforts, but so that we will turn to Him for help.

The longer we put off this step of surrender, the more trials will seem to focus on this Achilles heel. Finally, when we can't take it any longer, we will turn to God in absolute desperation. Then we'll discover, like Paul, that God does indeed delight in making His power perfect in our weaknesses. True spiritual maturity comes, not as I grow stronger in the Lord but as *God's power increases in me.*

As we learn this we can delight in weaknesses, in insults, in hardships, in persecutions, in difficulties, "For when I am weak, then I am strong." We can truly "consider it pure joy" as we face trials of many kinds. When we learn to delight in our weaknesses, knowing that in them God will manifest His strength, then we will have little trouble allowing Him to finish the work He has begun in us, bringing us to maturity.

Knowing all of the above, I am still left with one question for God: How long is this leg of the journey? How long will it take for all my rough edges to be chipped away and for me to truly be like Christ? I think it's a fair question, one that crosses all of our minds. Based on how long it takes the human species to grow to physical maturity, we know the process isn't short. There are no overnight spiritual giants. But how long could it really take?

The answer, unfortunately, is a lifetime. Listen closely to Paul's words to the church in Philippi in Philippians 3:12–14:

> Not that I have already obtained all this, or have already been made perfect, but I press on to take hold of that for which Christ Jesus took hold of me. Brothers, I do not consider myself yet to have taken hold of it. But one thing I do: Forgetting what is behind and straining toward what is ahead, I press on toward the goal to win the prize for which God has called me heavenward in Christ Jesus.

After serving the Lord for more than twenty years, Paul still felt that he had a long way to go. "Not that I have already obtained all this"—I haven't yet arrived at that point where I can say God is finished with me.

Paul was painfully aware of the truth that the farther we go with the Lord, the more clearly we can see how much longer the journey will be. The reason the process takes so long is the standard we press toward, Jesus Christ. If we were being measured against the world, the process would be short. If we were comparing ourselves to other Christians, it would take a little longer, depending on who we chose to compare ourselves to. Even if we went the extra mile and chose someone like Billy Graham as our standard, we could someday say that we had arrived. But when Jesus Christ is the standard, we will never fully arrive until the day we stand in His presence in heaven.

Verse fifteen of Philippians chapter three instructs us that all who are mature should share this same mind-set. Thus as we look back on the road we've already traveled, we see how much God has done up to this point. As we look ahead we see how much further we have to go. The hunger to continue pressing on is a sign that God is achieving His goal and that you are drawing closer to the place called maturity.

NOTE

1. C. S. Lewis, *The Problem of Pain* (New York: Macmillan, 1962), 96.

Travel Log:

*1. You and I are living stones that God reshapes in the image of His Son. I'm not sure if He chose that analogy because of the wonderful things an artist can craft from stone or because most of us tend to be hard to work with and a little rough around the edges. What are the rough edges God is chipping away from your life?*_____

_____

*How has He made you aware of them, and what chisel has He selected to do the job?*_____

_____

*How effective have His efforts been?*_____

_____

*Has the process been painful, and if so, why?*_____

_____

*Are you cooperating with His efforts or resisting them?*_____

_____

2. In Romans chapter five we find three stages of the journey toward the place called maturity: perseverance, character, and hope. While all three are simultaneous projects, we often find God concentrating on one over the others. Which of these three is He developing in you today? _____

Let me assure you, He is focusing on at least one of them. Every day the journey continues He wants to bring us closer and closer to this destination. Are you progressing today or have you stopped to relax?

_____

How satisfied are you with the progress God has made thus far?

_____

3. We focused upon trials and testing as "entrance exams to the next level of spiritual maturity." Usually they come upon us like a pop quiz, arriving when we least expect them. *What entrance exams have you taken lately?*_____

_____

*Were you prepared or did they take you by surprise?*_____

_____

How did you do on the last test you went through? What grade did you get? _____

*I know that sounds like an odd question, but think about it for a moment. What was God trying to accomplish?*_____

_____

*Was He successful?*_____

*Did it move you closer to your destination, or will you have to take a re-test?*_____

Our goal is to put on the character of Christ. With that as our standard, all of us still have a long trip ahead of us.

Chapter Six

TRIPPED UP BY QUESTIONS

I saw a picture one morning while reading the paper with breakfast that would have disturbed me greatly if I had given it time. It was of a small child, about the same age as my oldest daughter. The difference between my child and the one in the picture is the nations in which they live. While my family lives in a land of plenty, the farm belt of Indiana, this child had the misfortune of being born in East Africa. Her sunken eyes, swollen stomach, and pencil-thin limbs said more than I wanted to hear. Before the full impact of her suffering could leap off the page, I quickly turned past it. It's hard to enjoy the "breakfast of champions" looking into the eyes of one who probably will not awaken one morning in the not too distant future.

I'm not a cold or heartless person. I'm a lot like you. Images like this disturb me. They bring suffering into my dining room while giving me few options to alleviate it. But that isn't the only thing that disturbs me. A bigger question comes to mind, one that I hesitate to entertain for more than a few moments at a time: Looking into the eyes of the child in the photograph I wonder why God doesn't do something. Skeptics like to throw this question in the face of Christians, "Where is your God when innocent children starve to death?" But I'm not a skeptic. I've been a Christian since I was the age of the child in the photograph. I know the Sunday school answers, but the question haunts me just the same.

Following Jesus doesn't mean blindly accepting everything that happens in our world as "God's perfect will." Nor does it mean putting our brains on hold and ignoring the issues that suffering and injustice raise. This is an important point for understanding who we are as Christians and the journey of faith. Asking hard questions isn't blasphemy. Lightning won't come down out of the sky and strike you dead for reading these pages and giving serious thought to these issues. Others have asked the same questions and lived.

The fact is, when we ask where is God when innocents suffer or when life is unjust, we are recognizing that a world full of evil and suffering is a corrupted creation. God grieves the results of the Fall along with us. Habakkuk cried out, "How long, O Lord," shortly before Babylon came and carried Judah off into exile.

> How long, O Lord, must I call for help,
> but you do not listen?
> Or cry out to you, "Violence!"
> but you do not save?
> Why do you make me look at injustice?
> Why do you tolerate wrong?
> Destruction and violence are before me;
> there is strife, and conflict abounds.
> Therefore the law is paralyzed,
> and justice never prevails.
> The wicked hem in the righteous,
> so that justice is perverted. (Habakkuk 1:2-4)

In a word Habakkuk is crying out, "Lord, what on earth is going on? Where are You while our world falls apart? Do something, God! Do something fast!" God didn't strike him down for asking the hard questions the skeptics usually ask. The Lord gave an honest answer. To paraphrase, He told Habakkuk that He knew exactly what was going on and that He was in control. What's more, the nation of Judah could look forward to the situation proceeding from bad to worse. An army from a godless and wicked nation would soon sweep across their borders and carry them into exile. Habakkuk didn't get the answer he was looking for.

THE PROBLEM OF PAIN

Why doesn't God bring about justice on the earth? Where is He when innocents suffer and when life is unfair? The question exists because of one unpleasant fact of life that the human race has brought upon itself: Sin exists, and with it come pain and suffering. It's a package deal. No doubt there was some sort of discomfort in the world before the entrance of sin. We can safely conclude this on the basis of the Lord's statement to Eve that her pain in childbirth would be greatly increased. The difference in pain before and after sin's entrance is in its degree, not in its existence. Prior to the Fall the only pain was what C. S. Lewis described in *The Problem of Pain* as Type A pain, the useful sensation that tells us to remove our hand from a flame before the tissue is damaged. It poses no philosophical problems, because it is necessary for our existence. It warns us of danger and spares us from greater harm.

Yet the pain with which we are wrestling in this context was unknown to the couple in the garden. A world that was declared very good had no room for it. Adam and Eve didn't suffer separation anxiety when the Lord wasn't in their sight in the garden. There was no worry as to whether Eden's crops would fail, no thought of impending doom or disaster. Death was a completely foreign concept. The couple's focus was on life, life that was to be enjoyed and lived to its fullest extent in fellowship with the Creator. Their innocence didn't last long. The serpent slithered into paradise, deceived them both, and plunged the human race into its present state.

To a large part this explains why we question the existence of pain and suffering today. We weren't created for it. It was never meant to be a part of the human experience. The pain and sorrow we feel when a loved one dies testifies that death is an intruder into the world God created. The horror that fills our hearts as we view the innocents of the world suffering tells us that things aren't as they should be. Creation is out of order.

Knowing why suffering exists isn't enough when it strikes close to home. I was asking God "why?" as I walked into a hospital room in Visalia, California, one summer morning in 1992. I was there to see a woman named Ruth Smith. She and her husband had served together as home missionaries with the Southern Baptist Convention for more than twenty years. She was a very unassuming woman, a classic example of what the writer of the book of Proverbs had in mind when he penned the final chapter of that book. To say that she was faithful was an understatement.

But on this day it appeared that her times of service were over. The preceding summer the doctors told her she had inoperable lung cancer. We all thought that was impossible. She'd never smoked or done anything else normally associated with this disease. What followed was one agonizing round of chemotherapy after another, with all the usual side effects. As I went to see her that morning even this treatment had been abandoned. There was little more the doctors could do but wait for the inevitable.

I was praying about what I could say to comfort her or give her hope. Quickly I discovered that God had me there to listen, not talk. Ruth was sitting in her room waiting for the orderlies to finish changing the linen. Other than her hair, there was nothing in her appearance to indicate that anything was wrong. Peace radiated from her. She began to tell me how thankful she was that God had allowed her to walk down the path of suffering this disease brought on. "I've always been a Martha, too busy serving to take the time to sit at the feet of Jesus," she said, "but God has used this cancer to slow me down so that I can get to know Him in ways I never did before." I was asking God why she had to suffer; she was thanking Him for the experience! She also told me that God had given her a new ministry to other cancer patients. Many of them weren't ready to die. They were angry and frightened. God used this suffering servant to calm their fears and give them hope.

THE SECRET

I still ask why this disease has to continue, why it was ever invented in the first place. Yet I discovered that God is greater than any tumor. In Ruth Smith I saw firsthand what God does instead of ending all suffering: *He shares it.*

> Since the children have flesh and blood, he too shared in their humanity so that by his death he might destroy him who holds the power of death—that is, the devil—and free those who all their lives were held in slavery by their fear of death. . . . For this reason he had to be made like his brothers in every way, in order that he might become a merciful and faithful high priest in service to God, and that he might make atonement for the sins of the people. Because he himself suffered when he was tempted, he is able to help those who are being tempted. (Hebrews 2:14–15, 17–18)

The incarnation of Jesus Christ tells us more than God's eternal plan of salvation. It tells us of the mercy of God that moved Him to share in the plight of His people. Jesus' passion encompassed more than His final week. It was His way of life. Isaiah prophesied that He would be a man of sorrows and familiar with suffering. He knew both physical and emotional pain. Rejected by men, He was considered as one stricken by God.

Why was this necessary? Because of His suffering He is now able to come to the aid of those who suffer. We may endure pain, but in Christ we never endure it alone. When trials strike, we can pray to One who knows exactly how we feel. He's been there. This is true even in the things we think God cannot understand, like the pain we feel when one we love is taken in death. The shortest verse of the Bible, "Jesus wept," occurred at the tomb of a friend. He knows how we feel.

MORE QUESTIONS

Even so, the questions still haunt me. The suffering that children have to endure makes me call God's fairness into question. The newspapers are full of stories of children all over the world who live with death and suffering every day. Not all of these are located in the third world. Recently I read of twin two-year-olds whose mother died. While this is traumatic enough for anyone of any age, these toddlers had to endure even more. You see, their mother was a single parent, and she died while home alone with her children. Her body wasn't discovered for nine days. For those nine days two small, bewildered children tried to awaken their mother. They tugged on her arms, cried for her attention. Somehow they survived. Investigators said the inside of the house looked like a tornado had struck. Empty cereal boxes and food scraps were strewn all about. When people did finally go into the house they found the dead woman lying in bed with her two small children lying beside her, trying to keep warm.

As I look into the eyes of my three daughters, I wonder why these two innocents had to suffer this kind of trauma. My heart breaks thinking about what must have gone through their minds for that week and a half. Things like this just should not happen.

I hope at this point you haven't branded me a cynic. I can assure you that I am not. But I am human, and God's ways are beyond my comprehension, so I wrestle with these questions. Our world does too. Polls show that many Americans think the church is no longer relevant. Could it be that it's not the questions the world is asking that cause our problem but the answers we offer? "All you need to do is read the Bible and pray and all of these things will be taken care of" doesn't address the deeper hurts people around us are experiencing. If we never think through the skeptics' questions, how can we ever give a credible answer?

This is also true of the age-old question that we still raise today: Why does evil seem to triumph over good? Why does injustice run rampant in our world? Everything would be so simple if every evil act received immediate divine retribution. In Acts 12 we read how Herod was struck by an angel and eaten by worms when he allowed the crowds to praise him as a god. Think about what the world would be like if everyone received the King Herod treatment. Lightning would flash all around us striking down thieves, liars, rapists, and murderers. No one would get away with anything.

The only problem with such a world is that I'm allergic to lightning. The Bible's insistence that all of us are sinners means that each one of us would be struck dead in a world where swift justice reigned supreme. But even though we don't really want a world where justice reigns exclusively, we would like to see it assert itself a little more forcefully.

Nowhere is injustice more rampant than in the country of Bosnia in what was Yugoslavia. In the name of ethnic cleansing, thousands of innocent Muslim women are being brutally raped by the Serbian army. I recently watched a report from the front lines that only a cold and calloused heart could ignore. The television camera revealed a young woman in her early twenties whose life had been destroyed when she was gang-raped by more than fifty soldiers. Hatred had so blinded them that they became animals, not men. Now the first of what will most likely be thousands of children are being born to these women, only to be abandoned. Their mothers look at them and see only the hatred of the conquerors. The identities of the fathers are completely unknown. The cycle of injustice is picking up steam. At the time of this writing it looks as though nothing will be able to stop it.

Where is God while all of this is going on? Where is He when injustice reigns and innocents suffer? He is where He was before this present state was ushered in by our sin, on His throne reigning over the universe. These questions don't cause God to wring His hands worrying about what to do next. The problem we face is one of perspective. We're looking at the middle of the story as if it were the final chapter. There will be a day when justice will prevail and God will set all the wrongs right. But until that day we, like Habakkuk, must wait patiently and trust that God indeed knows what is best.

The Present Restraint of Evil

I also believe that as we ask God why things are so bad, we are missing the point on how bad things could become. Second Thessalonians 2:7 indicates that the Holy Spirit is restraining the power of evil during this present age. He truly is sovereign over our world that seems to be spinning out of control. If all this is true, then imagine for a moment what our world would be like if God wasn't a God of love or if He could somehow cease to be sovereign. Think of the horrors that our lives would be filled with if sin and all its salesmen had a free hand to do anything they desired.

The twentieth century has experienced small glimpses into what such a world would be like. One of the most chilling but forgotten examples took place in Indo-China in the late 1970s in the small country of Cambodia. Days after the Americans pulled out of the capital, Phnom Penh, the Khmer Rouge entered and began a reign of terror that left some 3 million of their own countrymen dead. Through a program of social engineering reminiscent of Joseph Stalin, this group of illiterate peasants set out to destroy everything about the past and achieve a total social revolution. Every city was emptied, and those who refused to leave were killed. Undesirables were systematically executed, including doctors, lawyers, civil servants, teachers, students, the poor, and the infirm. The bodies were piled into heaps in the countryside, the infamous killing fields. All of this was done publicly. Families were forced to watch as brothers, sisters, mothers, and fathers were butchered. Sometimes entire families died together.

The most frightening aspect of the cruelties of the Khmer Rouge is that the perpetrators were left unpunished. For the most part, the world was unaware or did not care what was taking place in the jungles so far from the Western world. Unlike Hitler's Germany, the world did not rise up together to take action. When the Khmer Rouge was overthrown by Vietnam, its leaders quietly slipped into the jungles to await another opportunity. There were no Nüremberg trials, no war crimes tribunals, just the stark realization that there is no limit to the cruelty man can perpetrate against his fellowman.

Evil in Earth's History

Ours is not the first generation to see such atrocities. History is filled with examples. One that took place in Jerusalem during the ministry of Jesus is alluded to in Luke 13. Luke doesn't go into detail regarding the particulars of the incident. Apparently a group of eighteen Galilean Jews had gone up to the temple to offer the ritual sacrifices the Law demanded. This was hardly a noteworthy occurrence, for it happened every day. But while this group was offering their sacrifices, Pilate ordered his soldiers to attack. All eighteen worshipers were mercilessly killed.

The incident is brought to our attention when someone came

to Jesus asking Him why it occurred. The person wanted to know how God could allow such a thing to happen and what Jesus was going to do about it. Here was the Messiah, the deliverer, from the city of Nazareth in the region of Galilee. Surely He would do something to avenge the lives of His fellow Galileans. If nothing else He could offer an explanation as to why God allowed Pilate to do such a thing and when Pilate would receive his just reward. Perhaps Jesus could give some insight into the terrible sins that these eighteen must have committed to force God to turn them over to such a horrible fate.

Jesus' reply is not what we might expect: "Do you think that these Galileans were worse sinners than all the other Galileans because they suffered this way? I tell you, no!" (Luke 13:2–3a). One mystery was solved. These men were not being paid back by God for some secret, dark, and terrible sin. Therefore, we can assume that God is going to take action and bring about swift justice, right? Wrong. Jesus continued, "But unless you repent, you too will all perish" (v. 3b).

Commentators are divided as to how to take these words. There is so little explanation of the events that they refer to that it is hard to draw any conclusions as to the type of perishing Jesus was referring to. Was He speaking to the Jews as a nation, warning them of the impending destruction by the Romans of A.D. 70 that came thirty years later? Or was He speaking to individuals, warning them of the uncertainty of life and the possibility of being ushered into eternity at any moment? Whatever His primary meaning, one thing is clear: Injustices like the fate of the eighteen Galileans are to be expected, then and now.

The rapid increase in technology in the latter years of our century has multiplied the potential harm that man can bestow upon his fellowman. We haven't seen the last of the killing fields. Injustice and cruelty will continue to raise their heads until the day that Christ returns. In the midst of it all we need to keep a proper perspective, one that has God securely upon His throne. If not for that, mankind as a species would probably have destroyed itself by now.

Knowing all of this, I still ask what I would say to the child whose picture invaded the tranquility of my breakfast. What hope could I offer if she physically came into my dining room? I couldn't give her a quick fix to the problems in her country. Nothing I could do would stop the killing. Would she believe me if I told her that God loves her? Perhaps she would if I showed her God's love. The questions we've wrestled with at this stage of the journey are more than discussion starters. They call us to imitate our Lord and share the hurts of those around us.

Travel Log:

*1. Walking by faith doesn't mean blindly accepting everything that happens as "God's perfect will" or ignoring the tough issues that suffering and injustice raise. Your spirituality isn't suspect if the cold, cruel nature of our world causes you to wonder if God is really in control. We need to wrestle with these questions, and the people around us also do. Have you witnessed anything lately, either personally or through the media, that makes you question God's goodness and mercy?*_____

_____

*What answers have people given to you or have you given to others when they ask you, "Why did God let this happen?"*_____

_____

*2. If you don't remember anything else from this chapter, please remember this: Rather than end all suffering, God shares it. Yes, He is able to wipe out everything bad. But He has chosen to display His power through weakness and share the suffering of those He loves. How does He share suffering in our world today?*_____

_____

Think about this for a while. What are some real, tangible ways you have observed God in action sharing the pain of His children?

_____

*Why would He choose this option rather than ending all suffering right now, today?*_____

_____

3. Put yourself in the position I described in the opening and closing *paragraphs of the chapter. What would you say to the young girl suffering from starvation?*_____

_____

*More importantly, what will you do for her and the millions like her?*_____

_____

There are no easy answers.

Chapter Seven

YOU WANT
ME TO
GO WHERE?!

"The Word became flesh and made his dwelling among us" (John 1:14). With this simple phrase God answers the skeptics who keep asking what He plans to do about the mess this world is in. As we found in the last chapter, God doesn't end all suffering. He shares it. But the Incarnation didn't end the day Jesus ascended into heaven. God still takes on flesh and comes to the aid of those in need. Only now the flesh He takes on is yours and mine. Welcome to our next destination on the journey of faith: ministry.

God calls every Christian to be a minister. Let me repeat that: God calls every Christian, everyone who claims to be a follower of Jesus Christ, to be a minister, a servant. I am convinced that one of the reasons the church in America has grown so weak is that we have forgotten this basic truth. We've made Christianity into a spectator sport where our primary responsibility is to sit in the stands and feel good while our team wins. God has a different idea. His plan for your life and mine is to involve us in the day-to-day work of His kingdom. The Holy Spirit constantly works to move us out of our comfort zones and into places where He can touch lives for eternity through us. Ordinary people like you and me, people full of fear and anxiety, people who have no idea where to begin—we're all part of His game plan. Ephesians 2:10 tells us that God has a lifetime of work already prepared for us, but first He has to get us ready.

PREPARATION

The paths God takes us down in this journey of faith are part of the preparation process. The trials, the struggles in prayer, the questions, the unpleasant surprises, all move us toward this destination. All along the way God moves us beyond ourselves by putting us in situations where we have to depend on Him alone. Like Israel during their wandering in the desert, many of the difficulties we face teach us lessons about our God that we couldn't learn any other way. Every experience we have may not be good, but they're all part of the process. God uses them for His ultimate good, preparing us for His service.

Four hundred thirty years before the Exodus, God began preparing a dreamer to save the world. Joseph was a man born for greatness. His brothers recognized it and hated him for it. All the essentials for leadership came naturally to him. Wisdom, insight, decisiveness—nothing was lacking. Yet Joseph's path to greatness took some unexpected twists and turns. His brothers dropped him in a deserted well because they despised him. Rather than kill him, they decided to sell him to the first travelers who came by. The man who would be savior found himself a slave in a foreign country. Just when it seemed that things couldn't get any worse he was thrown into prison, a victim of a scorned woman's lies.

While Joseph's life seemed to be spinning out of control, God was doing something unexpected. Through the fire of trials God was preparing a man who would take the world through seven years of famine. Because he had known little other than suffering, Joseph was the perfect man for the job. While everyone else panicked, he coolly guided Egypt as second in command to the king. As God's plan finally came into focus, Joseph was able to declare to his brothers, "And now, do not be distressed and do not be angry with yourselves for selling me here, because it was to save lives that God sent me ahead of you. . . . So then, it was not you who sent me here, but God" (Genesis 45:5, 8).

I don't think Joseph blindly accepted the years of suffering without becoming angry at God or asking Him why this was happening. His conversation with Pharaoh's baker and cupbearer reflects the demeanor of a man desperate to get out of jail. As the years dragged by he probably wondered if he would ever be free. The dreams of his childhood seemed like a cruel joke. But when the day of his deliverance finally came, he saw God's purpose in his suffering and counted it all as good.

Though we may never be sold into slavery by our brothers, God still uses similar methods to prepare us for the work He has in store for us. The key elements are the unexpected and the difficult, those things that push us beyond ourselves and test our faith. God isn't a sadist, deriving pleasure from making us miserable. But training camp is never easy. The more important the task, the more difficult the preparation. In the process God develops in us the things we need if we are to be successful in the work He calls us to do.

Endurance

The first essential God develops is endurance, the strength of character that sticks to a task even when it becomes difficult. Ministry is not glamorous. Its rewards are delayed, sometimes indefinitely, this side of eternity. People resist our noblest efforts to show Christ's love to them. Though we are working for the King, most of the work is done in obscurity among people the world hardly notices. Giving up can be a strong temptation.

Before He allows us to enter the fire God begins developing dogged determination in us. The process hurts because God is developing marathoners, not sprinters.

A friend once talked me into jogging with him in the mornings. I've never been much of a runner because, to be quite honest, I don't like the pain it causes or getting up early to do it. Besides, if I'm going to run, I need a reason, such as a large dog chasing me. But I finally said yes, I would be his new running partner. My goal was to get in shape, his goal was to compete in the Los Angeles Marathon. As my body began to ache, I gave up. My friend ran through the pain and not only competed but finished the race four consecutive years.

God has a job for every one of His children, some ministry that He wants you to do. Whether it's pastoring a church, teaching four-year-olds in Sunday school, or working with inner-city AIDS patients, the work is long and hard. It will never become easy or automatic. But when we become serious about being a Christian we'll find that we want to do that work more than anything else in the world. Thus, it's really an act of God's grace when He allows us to go through difficulties to develop the endurance we need to fulfill our calling.

Endurance alone isn't enough to serve effectively. Moses endured; he stayed on the job when anyone else would have quit. But something else made him a great servant of God. Numbers 12:3 says of him, "Now Moses was a very humble man, more humble than anyone else on the face of the earth." He was a leader, a judge, a writer, a shepherd. But above all things he was a humble servant.

Humility

Without humility no one can be an effective servant of God. In fact, no one will seek to serve God without it. There may be those individuals who enter "the Lord's service" with their pride intact, but they are serving themselves, not truly the Lord. Jesus didn't recruit personalities, He called people to deny themselves and follow Him. Listen to His words to the Twelve when He overheard them arguing about which of them was the greatest: "If anyone wants to be first, he must be the very last, and the servant of all" (Mark 9:35). Only the humble are in a position to have God work through them, for "God opposes the proud but gives grace to the humble."

Because humility is so vital to a servant of God, He will go to any lengths necessary to develop it in you and me. I find that those things that cause me the greatest embarrassment do me the greatest good because they reveal God's hand at work reshaping me as a servant. I'm not a masochist, nor do I suffer from a poor self-image. I don't enjoy being humiliated. But pride stops me from being usable by God. My home state has a saying, "It's hard to be humble when you're a Sooner." The human race could adopt this as our creed, "It's hard to humble, period." Therefore, when God helps us along the way by placing us in situations where we have to turn loose of our pride, He is doing us a great favor.

He doesn't just use bad things for this purpose. Many times direct obedience to God's plan will result in embarrassment. When I returned to seminary I uprooted my family and moved across country from California to Louisville, Kentucky. The only job I could find to support my family was mowing yards. There I was, a college graduate, an ordained minister with many years of experience, a published writer, doing the same thing I had done as a ten-year-old boy. By the end of each day I was covered with grass (and poison ivy) from head to toe, I was dirty, and I stank. God and I had a few conversations on those long, hot afternoons. Finally I had to ask Him what on earth was going on. Surely He could use me for something more productive than mowing yards.

The Lord replied with the words of Philippians 2:7, "[He] made himself nothing, taking the very nature of a servant." Jesus Christ became a servant for me. Now God was teaching me what it meant to be a servant for Him. Whether it be preaching, writing, or mowing yards, the thing that matters most to God is the condition of my heart. He does whatever it takes to set it right.

Dependence on God

The road to service also develops dependence upon God and God alone. The Israelites had nothing in the desert except what God gave them. Wal-Mart hadn't made it to the Sinai desert yet, and it's difficult to grow a garden when you're traveling continually. For forty years the nation without a country had to rely on God as their only hope. God's purpose was simple. He wanted them to learn that He was faithful so that they would continue to rely on Him when they arrived in Canaan.

I think this is the primary reason God uses difficulties to prepare us for service. He wants us to depend on Him for everything rather than depending on ourselves. Jesus said, "If a man remains in me and I in him, he will bear much fruit; apart from me you can do nothing" (John 15:5). All of our greatest plans for the kingdom of God will fail miserably when we forget this simple principle. *God isn't looking for people who will do great works for Him. He's looking for those He can do a great work through.*

The Lord also sets out to develop the other character qualities that a servant needs, such as patience, mercy, compassion, gentleness, and faithfulness. These may sound familiar. Paul lists nine such qualities in Galatians 5:22. We usually refer to them as the fruit of the Spirit. Sometimes we think that the Spirit drops these on us out of the blue, as though they automatically start blossoming from our lives. They don't. God develops them in us over time, like muscles. Bodybuilders don't create new muscles, they develop the ones we all have. In the same way, the Spirit creates a new person in us who has these qualities. As we travel down the road of obedience to Jesus Christ we'll find them developing and growing stronger. If patience is lacking, God places us in a situation that will allow it to develop (parents refer to this as the birth of their first child). If we're lacking compassion, the Lord allows us to go through situations that open our eyes to the needs and hurts of people around us.

Years of preparation don't do us any good until we begin to actually serve, to get our hands dirty (sometimes literally) in ministry. The transition isn't automatic. I've gone to school with a few people who can only be described as professional students. They're constantly moving from one degree program to another, changing majors and revising their life plans. Professional students prepare and prepare without ever moving out into the arena.

All of us could at times be classified as spiritual professional students. We read Christian books, listen to Christian radio, watch Christian television. From Evangelism Explosion to Navigator Bible studies, we've done it all. Some of us go the extra mile and support other ministries beyond our tithe or offerings to the church. But it all has a hollow ring if we stay cloistered in our safe Christian environment and fail to minister to those in need.

God calls every Christian to be a servant. What keeps us on the sidelines? We want to serve, but the prospect of stepping out of our comfort zones and doing something we've never done before can be very intimidating. All of our limitations scroll past our minds like a bad movie. Nothing is more frightening than thinking about actually trying to explain the gospel to another person. We get tongue-tied just thinking about it. And what if God wants us to go to a hospital or a nursing home? The smell alone makes us squeamish. Fear paralyzes us and keeps us on the sidelines out of the game. We want to serve, but where do we begin?

MINISTRY AND THE GLORY OF GOD

Before we can start ministering we need to know what Christian ministry is. Misunderstanding this basic concept paralyzes us or moves us in directions that are not biblical. Usually we think of ministry as something we go off and do. Missionaries and preachers surrender to "the ministry," then head off to seminary. Churches have children's ministries, youth ministries, women's ministries, men's ministries, ministries to shut-ins, ministries to the homeless, and on and on and on. They hire ministers to keep them running, who then try to talk us into volunteering our time. Other ministries exist independently of a local church. Many of them do a wonderful work with third-world orphans or unwed mothers.

All of this clouds the New Testament understanding of ministry and ministers. Ministers include all of us, not just a select few who earn their living from their work in the church. Nor is ministry something separate we do. For the Christian, it encompasses *everything* we do. Jesus' lordship extends over every aspect of our lives. Therefore, everything we do should be for His glory. In his first letter to the Corinthians Paul urged the church that "whatever you do, do it *all* for the glory of God" (1 Corinthians 10:31, italics added). Our goal in whatever we may do is to lift up and glorify the Lord Jesus Christ. But the scope of the command extends much further. He goes on in the next verses to say,

> Do not cause anyone to stumble, whether Jews, Greeks or the church of God—even as I try to please everybody in every way. For I am not seeking my own good but the good of many, so that they may be saved. Follow my example, as I follow the example of Christ. (10:32–11:1)

Glorifying Christ means to have a special concern for others, especially in seeking to win them to the kingdom. Note again how Paul doesn't instruct them to do this in their religious activities or in the specially sanctioned outreach services of the church. "Whatever you do, do it all for the glory of God."

Jesus expressed the same idea in His final words to the apostles before His Ascension, the Great Commission of Matthew 28:19–20. The New International Version follows most English translations by rendering the second word of verse 19 as a command: *go!* But a better translation would be "as you are going." The difference is substantial. Jesus aims His words at all of us to make disciples wherever we are, in the normal patterns of life. The New Testament records few missionaries who actually traveled around preaching the gospel. In spite of this, Christianity spread throughout the empire. Paul preached to small groups in the cities he visited. Yet the number of disciples multiplied. How? Believers made disciples as they were going through the marketplace, as they interacted with neighbors, as they went about the daily business of life.

This concept of ministry liberates us, changing the way we look at our jobs, where we live, and the daily routine we go through. Jesus is Lord, the Spirit is our guide. Therefore, we can trust God to move us in our daily pattern of life to the divine appointments He has for us each day. We don't necessarily need to go off to a distant mission field to get started. We simply need to recognize the mission field right outside our own door. Now "do it all for the glory of God."

Once we begin to see our entire lives as an avenue for ministry, opportunities to serve will come across our paths. Perhaps the one man best known for an opportunity coming across his path was the Good Samaritan. One day while walking along the road to Jericho he came across a broken heap of flesh, a Jew at the point of death. Earlier in the day thieves had ambushed the man and left him for the vultures. A priest and a Levite found him before the Samaritan, but they did their best to ignore him. Luckily for the injured man, the Samaritan cared enough to drop everything and help him.

MINISTRY AND HUMAN NEED

Jesus shocked His listeners with this tale of a religious outsider, a heathen, keeping the second greatest commandment while two religious leaders ignored it. Nothing in the story indicates the Samaritan feared God or lived by the law. But when faced with a fellow human being in need, he acted.

God regularly brings these kinds of situations across our path.

Often we are in such a hurry to get to one place or another that we never notice. Or the person in need may not fit the mold of the kind of people we associate with or who attend our church. It could be that we simply aren't willing to get our hands dirty and risk giving of ourselves to help. The opportunities are there. We need to open our eyes so that we can see them.

I think this is one of the reasons that God uses personal tragedies to prepare us to serve. Nothing makes us notice people in need like walking through the same trial ourselves. Going through the painful experience of my parents' divorce when I was ten has made me more sensitive to the needs of children caught in the same situation. Knowing what it was like to see my father walk out the door, suitcase in hand, makes me hurt for others who are going through the same situation. But more than that, having experienced God's grace in the midst of the pain, I can offer encouragement and hope. Paul summed it up best when he wrote, God "comforts us in all our troubles, so that we can comfort those in any trouble with the comfort we ourselves have received from God" (2 Corinthians 1:4). Not only do we have comfort to share with those who experience similar pain, our eyes are opened to the situation they face.

In addition to the daily opportunities to serve that God brings across our path, the Holy Spirit equips us for particular types of ministry through the spiritual gifts. All the gifts work for the common good, to enable the local body of Christ on earth, the church, to fulfill its calling. The Bible lists the gifts in broad, categorical terms rather than in specific job descriptions. Some of these include proclaiming the Word of God or prophesying, serving, teaching, encouragement, giving to the needs of others, leadership, mercy, faith, and discernment. In addition, God gives us talents that also need to be used for His glory. The ways in which these can be applied to serve God and the people around us are limited only by our imagination and the Holy Spirit's leadership.

Finding a Ministry That Fits

We may still find ourselves wondering specifically what we should be doing. How do we discover our gifts and our niche in the work of the kingdom? To this I would like to respond with two questions. First, what do you enjoy doing? Our gifts and talents usually lead us to God's plan for our lives. He also lays burdens upon our hearts for specific people and needs. Who do you hurt for? What needs do you see that no one else notices? God may well be showing you His will for your life. I also encourage you to experiment. Don't worry about specializing too quickly. Go to a prison for a weekend with Prison Fellowship or the Bill Glass team. Volunteer for the nursery one Sunday. Visit a nursing home or any other place where lonely people need a smiling face and an encouraging word. As you sample the opportunities before you, you'll find where God wants you to be. And use your imagination. God may be moving you to break the mold and start ministering to people in a whole new way. As I said before, the only limits are your imagination and the leadership of the Holy Spirit.

I hope you've grasped at least a small part of the excitement that this stop along the journey of faith holds for you. Nothing, absolutely nothing, compares with the joy of being used by God to touch another person's life for eternity. It's more addictive than heroin; once you start you won't be able to stop.

Three Pictures of Ministry

One word of caution: Being a servant is not all fun and games. It is hard work. In Paul's second letter to Timothy he uses three metaphors to paint a picture of ministry as a long, hard, difficult task:

> Endure hardship with us like a good soldier of Christ Jesus. No one serving as a soldier gets involved in civilian affairs—he wants to please his commanding officer. Similarly, if anyone competes as an athlete, he does not receive the victor's crown unless he competes according to the rules. The hardworking farmer should be the first to receive a share of the crops. Reflect on what I am saying, for the Lord will give you insight into all this. (2 Timothy 2:3–7)

The first is the picture of a soldier. The work of the Roman legions is legendary. They marched around the known world, defeating armies and conquering kingdoms without any modern machines of war. Battles were engaged hand to hand. Only the strong survived. Because of the demands of military service, no soldier could afford to have his attention divided. Civilian affairs would have to wait; all of the soldier's attention had to be devoted to the campaign at hand. Paul used this picture time and again to describe our task in taking the gospel around the world. Hardships lie ahead, and the enemy refuses to surrender.

The second picture is that of an athlete: Success on the athletic field comes through rigorous discipline and constant training. Natural gifts aren't enough. They have to be developed along with endurance. My memories of junior and senior high sports are of early morning workouts, wind sprints, weights, and constant laps around the gym. The glory on the field hardly compared with all the work that it took to get there. This same kind of hard, disciplined work awaits us in ministry. There's little glory but lots of sweat.

Paul's final picture is of a farmer. Farming not only illustrates the hard work necessary for successful ministry, it also shows how the rewards we work toward are usually delayed. Farmers work all year on the same plot of ground. Plowing, planting, weeding—the work never stops. From early in the morning to late at night, summer and winter, it's more than a job, it's a way of life. Yet the farmer has to wait and wait and wait to see any fruit from his labors. He also faces the uncertainty of what may happen to the crop.

A few years ago I lived across the road from an orange grove in California. The owner had been battling a four-year drought to try to bring in a crop. Just as the oranges were ripe enough to pick, the worst freeze in more than fifty years struck and wiped out more than 80 percent of his crop. That is ministry. The work is long and hard, the rewards are always delayed, and at any moment something may come along and wipe out all our work. Be strong in grace and endure to the end.

The hard work of ministry may also result in suffering. Listen to the ministry Jesus told Ananias He had prepared for Paul:

> This man is my chosen instrument to carry my name before the Gentiles and their kings and before the people of Israel. I will show him how much he must suffer for my name. (Acts 9:15–16)

The first sentence sounds like an exciting adventure. Who wouldn't want the opportunity to travel around the world, visiting exotic places, meeting kings, being accompanied by God Himself? Where do I sign up? But note the second part of the equation, suffering for the name of Christ. Becoming a servant meant Paul would face adversity on a daily basis. He wasn't alone. John Stott in his classic work, *The Cross of Christ*, says that suffering is indispensable for effective service.

> The place of suffering in service and of passion in mission is hardly ever taught today. But the greatest single secret of evangelistic or missionary effectiveness is the willingness to suffer and die. It may be a death to popularity (by faithfully preaching the unpopular biblical gospel), or to pride (by the use of modest methods in reliance on the Holy Spirit), or to racial and national prejudice (by identification with another culture), or to material comfort (by adopting a simple lifestyle). But the servant must suffer if he is to bring light to the nations, and the seed must die if it is to multiply.[1]

Becoming a servant not only means facing suffering; effective service demands it.

The Impulse to Quit

In the face of hard work and suffering it's easy to see why discouragement also comes with ministry. All of us find ourselves wanting to give up, to leave the game and never return. The strange thing is how discouragement often follows times of great victory. Elijah got discouraged one day and was ready to quit. He was tired of running from the evil queen Jezebel, he was tired of being the only prophet willing to stand up for God, he was tired of Israel's indecision about which god to serve. Overall, he was just tired. We find him sitting under a tree telling God to take his life, just days after defeating the prophets of Baal and calling fire down from the sky.

I've felt like Elijah some days. There are times that I want to run away to the mountains and never come back. But God gives us hope. He told Elijah to take a nap. After he caught up on his sleep, the prophet was able to hear God's next set of instructions.

The work we face is long and tiring. What a wonderful

thought to know that God never leaves us alone. As He told Jeremiah, His compassions never fail but they are new every morning. During those times we want to give up, God comes to our side and gives us the strength to face another day.

The Rewards of Sticking with It

Being a servant also brings great rewards. Joy, fulfillment, peace, happiness are just a few of its benefits. We also experience fellowship with God as He works through us. That deep fellowship cannot be experienced any other way. Yes, the work is hard. But all the hardships are worth it. As Paul said at the end of his life:

> I have fought the good fight, I have finished the race, I have kept the faith. Now there is in store for me the crown of righteousness, which the Lord, the righteous Judge, will award me on that day—and not only to me, but also to all who have longed for his appearing. (2 Timothy 4:7–8)

The abundant life Jesus calls us to is waiting for you at the place of service. You'll never know what you are missing until you arrive. Once you get there, you'll wonder why you waited so long.

NOTE

1. John R. W. Stott, *The Cross of Christ* (Downers Grove, Ill.: InterVarsity, 1986), 322.

Travel Log:

*1. God wants you to be a servant. He already has something unique in mind for you to do. Moreover, His Spirit is working to move you to the place of service. What is God doing to prepare you for the work He wants you to do?*_____

_____

_____

How has the Holy Spirit orchestrated events to lead you in the past?

_____

*What role has adversity played in the preparation process?*_____

_____

If you are actively involved in ministry, what negative events in the past have become assets in the work you are now doing? _____

_____

*2. Maybe you are like I was when I first began thinking about doing "ministry." Somehow, I had convinced myself that God wanted me to do something I would not enjoy some place far away with people who would tax my ability to love. Through the years I've discovered something wonderful. God designs us ahead of time for the tasks He has prepared for us. You may be searching everywhere to find your "calling" without much success. The answer may be as close as your favorite activity. What do you enjoy doing?*_____

_____

Our gifts and talents often lead us to God's plan for our lives.

*He also lays burdens upon our hearts for specific people and needs. Who do you hurt for?*_____

_____

_____

*What needs do you see that no one else notices?*_____

_____

God may well be speaking to you, showing you His will for your life. What appeals for helpers at your local church has God been telling you to respond to?

*3. Few people actually get involved in hands-on ministry. Most are content to sit on the sidelines and watch. It's easy to make excuses. Life goes at such a hectic pace, there's no time left for anything beyond scratching out a living and spending an ever-decreasing amount of time with our families. The pressure hits all of us. Yet, as you follow the Lord you will find that He constantly leads to the destination of service. He calls each of us to serve and He leads us to opportunities. What keeps you from taking an active part in ministry?*_____

_____

*We always find the time for whatever we consider to be important. Does your priority list need to be rearranged to make the time to do what God is calling you to do?*_____

_____

Earlier I told you that standard Sunday school answers aren't allowed in our discussions. This applies here. Spend some time with God going over your schedule. What adjustments does He want you to make?

Chapter Eight

WATCH
YOUR STEP

*T*he serpent, a seductress, a roaring lion, a strong man, the lure of the crowd, wolves disguised as sheep, deception hiding under the cover of truth. The Bible uses many metaphors to describe the one hazard all of us will face along the journey of faith—temptation. Cain was warned that it was crouching around the bend, waiting to spring its trap on him. Solomon warned his son that it would come looking for him and that its appeal would be irresistible. Whatever form temptation may take, we know it is out there, waiting for us. Even more troubling, it also lives within us in the form of our own pride and evil desires, searching for our weaknesses.

When we set out to follow Jesus Christ, our lives undergo a radical transformation. The Bible speaks of this as a second birth, becoming a new creation. Not only do we experience forgiveness, we're liberated from the cycle of sin and alienation from God. In Christ we are free, free from sin and free to please God. We inherit a new nature re-created in the image of Jesus. Our desires change. Suddenly we find that we want to please

God. The old sinful habits lose their appeal, but not completely.

In Christ all things are made new, but we're still troubled by the lures of the old. Walking by faith doesn't make us immune to temptation. The flesh, our natural craving for sin, remains with us throughout our lives. God doesn't take it away when we accept Christ as Savior. Instead He breaks the flesh's power over us, thus making it possible for us to not give in to the tempter's lies. Only in Christ is there true freedom *not* to sin; but that doesn't imply a freedom from temptation. The path of faith enables us to say no to the desires of the flesh in order to say yes to the will of God.

TEMPTATION IN SCRIPTURE

You don't have to look very hard to find temptation in the Bible. It entered the drama of Scripture in the third chapter of Genesis and assumed a major role from that point forward. The first family continued to be plagued by it when Cain gave in to his anger and jealousy and killed his brother. By the sixth chapter of the Bible the entire human race was so corrupted by the influence of sin that God decided to get rid of everyone. Even after the Flood temptation remained a problem. Noah, the righteous shipbuilder, got drunk and created a family crisis. Later, Noah's descendants gave in to pride and built a monument for themselves at Babel. When God's plan of redemption narrowed to Abraham and his family, the story didn't change. From Abraham, to his children and grandchildren, to the nation that emerged from them, sin and temptation continually complicated lives.

In the New Testament the adversary, Satan, continued to weave his web of deception. He tempted Jesus in the wilderness, then hounded His ministry through the constant testing of the Pharisees. In Acts we find Ananias and Sapphira giving in to temptation and testing the Holy Spirit. The letters to the churches wouldn't have been written if it were not for the constant battles against the influence of the flesh and sin.

SUCCESSFUL TEMPTATION

Temptation continues to be so successful because it never changes. It sticks to the basics that have worked since the Garden of Eden. Usually it begins by making us dissatisfied with what we have. Adam and Eve had everything anyone could ask for. The entire world was at their feet. God gave it all to them with only one exception. The serpent played on the exception: He focused Eve's attention on the one plant God placed off limits, making her forget completely about the thousands of others that they could enjoy. What they had wasn't enough. They had to have the fruit from the forbidden tree.

We laugh at how gullible Adam and Eve were, without recognizing how often we fall into the same trap. We're driving down the highway in our 1984 Chevy, singing along with the radio, happy as can be. Then we notice a new convertible zip by with its sleek lines and shimmering paint. Suddenly, our countenance changes. We begin to notice every tear in our car's interior, every scratch on the hood. Even though our old car still runs well and completely meets our needs, it's not good enough anymore. We covet the car of a stranger and begin plotting how we can move up the ladder of automobile success. I'm not saying that buying a new car is a sin. Everything mechanical wears out and must be replaced. But when our decision is based on desire rather than need, it is a problem.

Dissatisfaction doesn't work alone. Before anyone will give in to temptation he has to believe that his action won't have any negative consequences. That is why the serpent's next line to Eve was, "You will not surely die. Nothing bad will happen. Trust me." I don't know why anyone would take the word of a snake. *How would he know that they wouldn't die?* Maybe Eve believed him because he was slithering around in the forbidden tree without being hit by a bolt of lightning. Maybe she fell for his lines because he told her exactly what she wanted to hear. Promising people whatever they want without any consequences has always been an easy way to win friends and influence people.

Our world specializes in trying to take the fear out of sin. Schools hand out condoms to remove the fear of disease and pregnancy from premarital sex. If the condom happens to fail, you can always have the simple procedure of abortion. The justice system is forced by overcrowded jails to release all but the worst lawbreakers (and even some of the worst), effectively removing the fear of punishment from many crimes. Society strives to accept any sort of lifestyle so that there is no longer any fear of being ostracized for living a life of perversion. Through it all our world scoffs at the concept of God and a judgment day. If God does exist, He wouldn't actually send anyone to hell. A popular talk show host proclaimed that her God loved everyone too much to do such a thing.

TEMPTATION FROM THE INSIDE

Temptation then moves to something much more personal. It appeals to our pride. "You will be like God," the serpent promised. We can almost hear the rest of the sentence, "Isn't that what you deserve?" The first couple saw their chance to escape their place as creatures and assert their sovereignty over the Creator. They ate of the fruit, not because the devil made them do it, but because they wanted what could only be gained by the fruit. It was desirable for gaining wisdom, for moving up to God's level.

This brings us face to face with one of the sad facts of sin. We do it because we want to. No one twists our arms and makes us take what doesn't belong to us. No one grabs our head and forces us to lust after the girl in the string bikini. We sin because we enjoy it. The act of sin takes on an irresistible charm and appeal. The forbidden fruit looked good for food, pleasing to the eye, and desirable to make one wise. Eve wanted it more than anything else on earth. So the woman ate and shared her prize with her husband.

The first man and woman had an advantage over the rest of us. Temptation was to them purely external. It played on their human nature, but the desire for sin didn't come from inside them. Before the Fall they lived in a state of innocence. Now the battleground of temptation has shifted from outside to inside us. Jesus said that all the evil that men do comes from within their fallen hearts. James tells us that our own evil desires drag us away and entice us to sin. The secret thoughts, the inward desires, plague us all of our lives. Snakes don't need to drop out of trees. We carry them around with us every day.

NO IMMUNITY AVAILABLE

When I say us, I mean all of us. No one is immune from sin. Not even the great heroes of the Bible were immune from temptation's influence. One story that ought to frighten all of us is

David and Bathsheba. David wasn't an ordinary man. God called him a man after His own heart. His prayers continue to speak today through the Psalms. Reading his poetry I find myself wondering if anyone knew God as intimately as King David.

One night David decided to stop praying and go for a walk on his rooftop. As he looked down he saw an incredibly beautiful woman taking a bath. Rather than turn away, he stopped and stared. Her beauty became more than he could bear. It didn't matter that she was the wife of one of David's soldiers. He had to have her and would not rest until she was brought into the palace. When David's desire produced a child he set out to hide what he had done. Unable to make it appear that Bathsheba's child belonged to her husband, Uriah the Hittite, David sent instructions to Joab to make sure that Uriah didn't survive the next battle. With her husband dead, David felt free to marry the woman of his desire.

If the man who penned the Twenty-third Psalm could sink to such depths, how much more susceptible to sin are you and I? No wonder Paul warned the church in Corinth, "If you think you are standing firm, be careful that you don't fall!" (1 Corinthians 10:12). All of us—no matter how long we've been Christians, regardless of how much we know about God and the Bible, in spite of any positions we may hold in the church—*all* of us are vulnerable to the tempter's lies.

Therefore, we need to be careful, to watch out, to do everything we can to protect ourselves from falling into sin. Just saying no isn't enough. In the heat of the moment temptation's offer can be overwhelming. Even the stoutest of heart find themselves wanting to give in. Nor can taking a strong stand against sin make us immune to its appeal. Prohibitions alone can actually stir up within us the desire to do what we despise. Paul stated in Romans 7 that focusing on the command not to covet produced in him every kind of covetous desire. No wonder the religious scandals of the mid-1980s were littered with preachers who specialized in condemning the very acts they were engaging in. If we are going to win the battle against temptation and walk in the freedom Jesus promised us, we need to develop the transformed attitudes that result in true freedom. These go beyond saying no to sin. They come through surrender to the lordship of Christ and the transforming power of the Holy Spirit.

THE GREATEST PROTECTION

The greatest defense we can build against temptation is the simple attitude of contentment. Temptation tells us we need more, that what we have doesn't measure up. Contentment replies that what we have is more than enough. It breaks the cycle of constantly wanting more stuff and newer toys by deciding to be satisfied. It also turns us from the apparent need to lust and manipulate to get our own way, because we know that we can be content in the circumstances God has placed in our lives. Paul spoke of contentment as the key to his surviving all the trials and travails he went through. Listen to his words to the church in Philippi:

> I rejoice greatly in the Lord that at last you have renewed your concern for me. Indeed, you have been concerned, but you had no opportunity to show it. I am not saying this because I am in need, for I have learned to be content whatever the circumstances. I know what it is to be in need, and I know what it is to have plenty. I have learned the secret of being content in any and every situation, whether well fed or hungry, whether living in plenty or in want. I can do everything through him who gives me strength. (Philippians 4:10–13)

We find in this passage some key characteristics of contentment. First, it operates independently of what one has. There is no minimum level of "stuff" required, no minimum standard of living necessary before we can be satisfied. Paul said "whatever situation." Good or bad, hungry or well fed, dressed in clothes from Neiman-Marcus or Wal-Mart (or even the Salvation Army), whatever we have is enough. Most of us fail at this point. We want to be content and we plan to be. But first we need to move into a bigger house, the old car needs to be replaced, there's a wonderful new appliance we just have to have, and on and on and on. As a result, the desire for stuff fills our prayers as we plead with God to provide what we absolutely *must* have. In contrast, a content heart happily accepts whatever it has without asking for more.

Hebrews 13:5 shows that choosing to be satisfied is also an act of faith.

Keep your lives free from the love of money and be content with what you have, because God has said, "Never will I leave you; never will I forsake you." So we say with confidence, "The Lord is my helper; I will not be afraid. What can man do to me?"

When we heed the command to be content, we are in essence saying, "God will provide everything I need. What I have must be what God thinks I need. Therefore I will trust Him and accept His provision." Though my flesh cries out for more, contentment comes as my flesh, my earthly desires, are crucified with Christ by faith.

Satisfaction

Accepting God's provision by faith makes us realize that giving thanks and rejoicing are integral parts of contentment. Just a few lines before Paul wrote of contentment in Philippians 4, he penned these words:

> Rejoice in the Lord always. I will say it again: Rejoice! Let your gentleness be evident to all. The Lord is near. Do not be anxious about anything, but in everything, by prayer and petition, with thanksgiving, present your requests to God. And the peace of God, which transcends all understanding, will guard your hearts and your minds in Christ Jesus. (vv. 4–7)

No wonder Paul could say that he was satisfied whatever his circumstances. Refusing to fret over what he did not have, he rejoiced and gave thanks for what he had. He didn't grudgingly mumble, "OK, God, I guess this is enough." No, he chose to rejoice and be genuinely happy about everything God gave him. Remember, the theme of the letter to the Philippians is joy— even though it was written from a jail cell. The more we say thank you to God with great joy, the more content we'll find ourselves becoming.

Learned Contentment

One final characteristic of contentment needs to be kept in mind. It doesn't drop down upon us from heaven one day, instantly transforming us like Scrooge in *The Christmas Carol*. Rather, it is a process we learn over time. Note that Paul said that he had *learned* to be content. He probably went through the same struggles you and I face in trying to put these words into practice. With time he learned the secret of relying on the Lord to provide his every need, giving him the freedom to rejoice whatever his circumstances. Discovering the secret of how to be content is really quite simple. The challenge comes in putting it into practice.

Contentment kept Paul from becoming bitter against the churches that seemed to forget him in his time of need. It gave him the freedom to serve without worrying about what he would receive in return. He accepted whatever situation he found himself in, whether good or bad. Paul wouldn't fit into our modern world. He refused to whine or call himself a victim. Instead he chose to be content. We too can choose to be content. When we do we'll find the same freedom Paul experienced, a freedom from sin and a freedom to serve. It will build a wall around our hearts that will make the tempter's song much less appealing.

HUMILITY

The second wall against temptation, humility, is closely related to the first. In the previous chapter we looked at how essential this quality is for those who seek to serve God. But a humble heart also protects us against the lure of temptation. James reminded his readers that: "'God opposes the proud but gives grace to the humble.' Submit yourselves, then, to God. Resist the devil, and he will flee from you" (James 4:6–7).

Temptation whispers that we should have it all; nothing is too good for us since we are the center of our universe. Humility silences the lies by gladly accepting our proper place before God as part of His creation and as those who have been redeemed by Jesus Christ. I like the word picture James draws. As we submit to God and say no to pride, the Devil has to run away. A humble heart is to the devil like kryptonite is to Superman.

Charles Swindoll simplified the whole idea of what it means to be humble in his book *Improving Your Serve:* "Genuine humility operates on a rather simple philosophy. Nothing to prove, nothing to lose."[1] I've found myself being rescued from many situations by reminding myself of these words. Nothing to prove: I don't have to try and impress those around me. Nothing to lose: Everything has already been lost to Jesus Christ. A humble heart also liberates me to forgive others freely just as God in Christ has forgiven me, thus breaking the cycle of sin.

Accountability

Making myself accountable to others puts humility into practice. It also protects me from temptation. All of us are ultimately accountable to God for our actions. Christians and non-Christians alike will someday stand before God to answer for all that we have done in this life. Judgment Day is a great equalizer. Revelation 20 paints a frightening picture of all the dead, from the greatest person who has ever lived to the poorest beggar who died in obscurity, standing before the Great White Throne of God, all equally guilty. Those of us who have found forgiveness in Christ are still accountable to our Savior for what we do with the new life He has given us. The thought of having to answer to someone is a sobering thought, one that can steer us away from wasting this life on the frivolous pursuits of sin.

Making oneself accountable to other people takes what is true before God and brings it down to a human scale. Eternity is a long way off, and God can seem very far removed when temptation begins to draw us into its web. But knowing that I am going to have to explain what I have done to a brother or sister in Christ awakens me to the consequences of the act I'm pondering. It's not easy exposing my weaknesses to friends, and at times people's nosy questions make me angry. Therefore, I'm very selective about the people I develop this kind of relationship with. Just as we know that the Savior who holds us accountable loves us, accountability on a human scale must be based on love. Nor does Christ go and parade my dirty laundry for the world to see. So too, an accountability partner must be able to be trusted with a confidence. But once a person has proven trustworthy in this capacity, I need to fight the tendency to make excuses for my behavior rather than change what he brings to my attention.

Accountability is essential on this journey. It gives us someone to call out to us when we stray off the path. As the writer of Ecclesiastes said, "Two are better than one, because they have a good return for their work: If one falls down, his friend can help him up. But pity the man who falls and has no one to help him up!" (Ecclesiastes 4:9–10).

Everyone falls from time to time. We need someone who loves us enough to stop and help us to our feet.

Avoiding the Source

Perhaps the simplest defense against sin is simply avoiding the source of temptation. I know this sounds obvious, sort of like the old joke, "Doctor, it hurts when I do this!" To which the doctor replies, "So don't do that." All of us find some particular sin harder to resist than any other. Therefore we need to know where our weaknesses lie and avoid them. A close friend of mine is a redeemed alcoholic. Even though several years have passed since his last drink, the temptation remains. Therefore, common sense dictates that my friend avoid places that serve alcohol and the situations that remind him of his drinking days. Drinking never appealed to me. I can't stand to be around drunks, and I don't like being out of control. My weakest point is worry. I come from a long line of worriers. In fact, if you look up the word in the dictionary you will find a copy of our family tree. The only difference between my worrying and my friend's drinking is that he doesn't engage in his pet sin anymore. They're both equally wrong. Thus, if I want to win the victory over worry I need to stop dwelling on the problems that kick my worry gene into high gear. Rather than worry, I must choose to pray.

I don't know where your weakness lies. It could be lust, coveting, anger, a critical spirit, lying, stealing, or any number of things. Facing your temptation head-on and fighting it may seem macho, but it will usually lead to defeat. Don't fight it, avoid it. Stop watching movies that stir up lust, stay away from the new car lots if they cause you to covet, avoid the crowd that brings out the worst in you. The flesh creates enough trouble on its own without being placed in situations where it can flourish. Understand what your flesh craves and stay away from it. It may sound simplistic, but it works.

Even if we avoid temptation as much as humanly possible, it will still come looking for us. God doesn't protect us from it; otherwise He would have to completely remove us from this world. Somehow the tempter manages to breach the walls of contentment, and discontentment tunnels under humility and sneaks past accountability to confront us face to face. In those moments where do we turn? Perhaps no verse has helped me like Paul's words to the church in Corinth:

> No temptation has seized you except what is common to man. And God is faithful; he will not let you be tempted beyond what you can bear. But when you are tempted, he will also provide a way out so that you can stand up under it. (1 Corinthians 10:13)

God gives us some wonderful words of reassurance and a life-saving promise in this verse. He begins by removing the isolation and shame we feel when we're tempted. Strange thoughts come into our minds, tempting us to do things that believers should never consider doing. There must be something wrong with us to even think of such things! But Paul tells us to relax; we're not the first individuals to go through this battle. Satan ran out of new tricks long ago. Other believers throughout time and throughout the world have faced the same battles we're fighting today.

What Has Worked Before

If other people have faced this same struggle, then part of an effective battle plan must be to learn what it took for them to be victorious. Generals don't dream up new war plans on their own. They look at the past and the methods that brought victory or sank an army in defeat. Learning from the past can mean military victory today. The battle we're engaged in is no less real. We can't see our adversary, but we know he's there. That is why it is so important for older believers to instruct the younger. Through their years of experience they can share the keys to success and help those who are less advanced on the journey to avoid traps that lead to failure.

GOD'S FAITHFULNESS

God also reassures us by reminding us that He is faithful. He hasn't forgotten about us, nor has He lost sight of His plan for our lives. In a word Paul is telling us to stop relying on our own willpower and cast ourselves on the faithfulness of God. James tells us that God can't be tempted by evil, nor does He tempt anyone to sin. Moreover, He has yet to lose a fight with the Devil. His record is unblemished. Just look at Jesus in the wilderness. Satan offered Him the entire world! Our Lord told him to get lost. The same One who was victorious in the wilderness is available to help us today. Our willpower falters, but His faithfulness never fails.

His final word to us is a promise: "He will not let you be tempted beyond what you can bear" (1 Corinthians 10:13). God is in control. He knows what you are going through; He sees how intense the desire is becoming. But He won't let it become so intense that falling is inevitable. How? By providing a way out, a secret escape hatch that sets you free. I find it interesting to realize how different God's methods are from our own. He does not give us more willpower or a firmer resolve to say no. Instead, He tells us to take the coward's way out and run away. If we stand under the tree with Adam and Eve long enough, we'll fall for the serpent's lies. God's solution is distance: Take the way of escape. He promises to provide the avenue; all we have to do is take it.

As I said at the beginning of this chapter, temptation awaits us on the road of faith. God doesn't kill all the serpents or take away all the desires of the flesh. But that doesn't leave us stranded in our old way of life, continually defeated by sin. On the cross sin and death were rendered a fatal blow. As we walk in the shadow of the cross, allowing God to put to death our old desires, we'll find that the victory of Christ's resurrection can be ours every day.

NOTE

1. Charles Swindoll, *Improving Your Serve: The Art of Unselfish Living* (Dallas: Word, 1981), 25.

Travel Log:

*1. Temptation strikes all of us. No one is immune—not you, not me, not the greatest heroes of the faith. All of us find ourselves in its unwelcome company. What areas of your life does the tempter usually strike?*_____

_____

*Sometimes our enemy knows us better than we know ourselves. Do you have one or two problem areas where it seems you are constantly failing?*_____

_____

Recognizing your weaknesses is the first step to victory.

*2. What defenses are you building to protect yourself from the tempter's appeal?*_____

_____

We looked at several walls each of us needs to build. Let's go back over a few of these.

How content are you? _____

*Specifically, are you satisfied with your car?*_____
*Your house?*_____ *The gadgets in your kitchen?*_____ *Your wardrobe?*_____

*We've talked a lot about pride in these pages. Let me ask you, how are you doing with humility?*_____

I know that is hard to answer. Let me try to make it easier. Can you honestly say that you have nothing to prove and nothing to lose? ____

_____

*Who are you accountable to?*_____

Do you have someone to ask you hard questions about your walk with the Lord? _____ *How often do you meet together?* _____

*3. In a later chapter we will discuss what to do when we stray from the path of faith. However, I feel I need to stop now and ask you, how are you doing in your battle against temptation?*_____

_____

Are you losing the fight?_____ If so, the Bible has a wonderful promise for you. First John chapter one, verse nine tells us that if we confess our sin, God will forgive us and set us free. Is there unconfessed sin in your life that you need to talk to God about right now?_____ The next chapter talks about fellowship with the Father, one of the sweetest destinations this journey holds. You'll never arrive if sin has come between you and God. Get alone with Him and set things right.

Chapter Nine

NEVER
ALONE

*I*t's a mystery I've never understood. The more I think about, it the more confused I become. I can accept it as a fact, but understanding why it is true is more than I can comprehend. A Sunday school teacher first told me of it many, many years ago. Later I found it in the Bible. But even the Bible doesn't explain it. Instead it presents it as a basic premise of the way God intended things to be since the beginning of time. My curiosity wants to know why God would do this and how something like this could be possible. Don't get me wrong. I'm not complaining. Quite the contrary. I am amazed because it is more wonderful than the human mind can comprehend. Just think of it: God, the mighty, wonderful, sovereign Creator of heaven and earth, wants to spend time with me. A lot of time, an eternity. And He works day after day to draw me closer to Himself in order that I might get to know Him better and that we might enjoy each other's company.

Because God wants intimate fellowship with you and me, we will never go through a moment in this journey when we are completely alone. Before He left this earth Jesus promised His follow-ers that He would never leave us nor forsake us, even to the end of the age. His words apply both to the original eleven men who watched Him ascend into heaven and to those of us who eagerly await His return. Having Jesus' presence is much more than car-rying His memory or remembering the words that He spoke. He sent the Holy Spirit to indwell every believer so that God Himself can walk with us each and every day. What an amazing concept.

The possibility of intimate fellowship with God didn't begin during Jesus' earthly ministry. We find it at the very beginning of time, with the creation of the first man and woman in the Gar-den of Eden. God created the human species in His image so that we could have a real relationship with Him. Dogs and cows aren't created in His image, nor do we find them carrying on conversations with the Lord. The image of God in mankind sets us apart. It allows us to relate to God, to know Him, and to be known by Him. We are able to experience His love and return it to Him freely. We can communicate with more than words and can know more of Him than ideas about who He is.

This kind of relationship doesn't come easily. Adam and Eve created the first barrier to fellowship with God, and all their descendants have repeated the process. That barrier is sin. Many times we think of the resulting separation as God's doing—He's the one who drove the first couple out of the Garden of Eden and out of His presence. But when we return to Eden we find Adam and Eve hiding from God long before He banished them. He didn't break off their relationship; Adam and Eve did. We're no different. Sin causes us to pull back from God, to hide from Him, to refuse His offer to have fellowship with Him. It sepa-rates us because we want it to.

Therefore, God intervenes to change hearts and draw people to Himself. He began this long ago with Abraham and Sarah. Through them He promised to give a blessing to the entire world, a blessing that culminated with the birth of Jesus. The greatest blessing God bestowed on them is found in Genesis 17. There God pledged to them that He would be their God and they would be His people. A new relationship entered the expe-rience of mankind, the experience of knowing God intimately and personally. Abraham and Sarah began living in a covenant relationship with God, a covenant God both initiated and guaranteed. For Abraham and Sarah, the climax of their relationship with God came in the birth of their son, Isaac. He was more than the fulfillment of a promise. Because of Isaac's impossible birth, God and a very surprised couple laughed together.

INTIMATE RELATIONSHIP

Moses knew this kind of intimacy with God, an intimacy the Lord desired with the rest of the nation He wanted to make a "kingdom of priests." The two of them spoke together face to face, like close friends. They shared their deepest feelings, Moses pouring out his complaints to God, the Lord telling Moses He was sick and tired of the stiff-necked Israelites. At times they became angry with each other, although the Lord always prevailed in their disputes. Their relationship endured to the end. On the day Moses died no one was present except the Lord. From high above the Jordan plain God showed Moses the land He had promised to Abraham, Isaac, and Jacob, the land that had been Moses' quest for the past forty years. After sharing a final moment together on earth, God ushered His servant into His presence forever.

The Psalms continue to guide many of us into the presence of God. David and the other writers describe a God so powerful and frightening that His words cause even the mountains to tremble. His enemies flee in terror before Him, and all creation shouts His praises. Yet He also draws close to His children and loves them with an undying love. One of my favorite psalms is Psalm 103, especially verses 11–14. Listen to the gentle, loving relationship God desires to have with you and me.

For as high as the heavens are above the earth,
so great is his love for those who fear him;
as far as the east is from the west,
so far has he removed our transgressions from us.
As a father has compassion on his children,
so the Lord has compassion on those who fear him;
for he knows how we are formed,
he remembers that we are dust.

I love the word picture David paints. It reminds me of what awaits us in heaven when God's relationship with us will be so intimate and personal that God Himself "will wipe every tear from their eyes" (Revelation 21:4).

I think of that every time one of my daughters comes to me in tears. Whether she has fallen and scraped her knee or is simply going through a very bad day, all she wants from her father is to be held close and assured that everything will be OK. She's not looking for answers, just a warm embrace that I happily give. God made us to have that same kind of relationship with Him. We can come to Him at any time and draw near to Him like a child draws near to a loving father.

What Fellowship Means

Many of us struggle with *how* to draw near to God on a regular basis. I know I do. Jesus left us an example to follow of taking time out on a regular basis to be alone with the Father. His times were devoted to prayer and seeking to know His Father's will. Most of us stay so busy that we fail to block out time each day to do nothing other than sit in God's presence and listen for His voice or to take the concerns of our heart before Him. But quiet times alone aren't enough. By themselves they soon become monotonous and their power slips away.

Another option we often choose is corporate worship with other believers. The goal of worship is ideally to praise and adore our God and Lord. The word *worship* means to ascribe worth and honor to His name. The songs we sing, the testimonies we share, communion, and the other elements of public worship are all designed to focus our attention upon our great and wonderful Lord. We come before Him as a group of believers, people who hold both a common faith and a common experience of forgiveness and rebirth, in order to lift Him up and adore Him. God promises to meet with us during these times. The psalmist says that God inhabits the praises of His people (Psalm 22:3). As we glorify His name we can sense the nearness of His Spirit.

But songs of worship and praise have a hollow ring without one other vital element of the Christian walk. Yes, we draw near to God through worship, both public and private. Yes, we draw near to Him through prayer and studying His Word. But there is more, something that is too often forgotten. Real fellowship with God also includes going out and doing what He commanded us to do. Earlier I referred to Jesus' parting words to His disciples, His promise to be with them even until the end of the age. We must remember the context of that promise. It comes on the heels of His command to them to go and make disciples. As we go and take the gospel to the world, Jesus Christ goes with us.

The church in Acts knew this concept well and lived it. The fourth chapter of Acts describes one of its worship services and prayer meetings. Scripture plays a prominent role. They all prayed together, apparently all at the same time and all aloud. Their primary requests were for the Lord to give them boldness to share the gospel and for God to work in a miraculous way in lifting up the name of Jesus. What an answer they received! God shook the room as He filled them with the Holy Spirit. Then they went out and preached the Word of God boldly. Later we read of Stephen being filled with the Holy Spirit and proclaiming the gospel even at the cost of his own life. In fact, being filled with the Holy Spirit and spreading the gospel always go hand in hand in the book of Acts. The Spirit provides more than power and boldness. He is God Himself drawing near to His servants and working through them to do what they could never do on their own. Because the work remains, Jesus' promise remains. As we go out into the world with the gospel, He goes with us, just like He said.

God's Initiative

Being close to God doesn't depend on our efforts alone. He takes the initiative to draw us near to Himself. His Holy Spirit creates a longing deep within our hearts for intimacy with the Father. Romans 8:15 calls Him the Spirit of sonship who causes us to cry out, "*Abba*, Father," the cry of a child for his father. He instills the love of God within our hearts, a love for others and especially a love for the Lord Himself. Apart from the Spirit's work we would never draw near to God. The remnants of sin in the flesh would continually pull us back from Him in fear. The Spirit crucifies the flesh and fills our hearts with a passion that can only be satisfied by God Himself. He creates an insatiable desire to know Him, a longing so great that everything else pales in comparison. Paul summed it up best in the third chapter of Philippians:

> But whatever was to my profit I now consider loss for the sake of Christ. What is more, I consider everything a loss compared to the surpassing greatness of knowing Christ Jesus my Lord, for whose sake I have lost all things. I consider them rubbish, that I may gain Christ. . . . I want to know Christ and the power of his resurrection and the fellowship of sharing in his sufferings, becoming like him in his death, and so, somehow, to attain to the resurrection from the dead. (Philippians 3:7–8, 10–11)

These words are only possible through the regenerating power of the Holy Spirit.

In spite of the Spirit's continual drawing, we still find ways to resist the Lord's advances. We fill our lives with activity and noise to such a degree that the Spirit's voice becomes lost in the crowd. It's not that we decide to stop spending time with God. The desire for fellowship with Him remains deep within our hearts. But we become so preoccupied with doing everything else that He is pushed out of our lives or relegated to one lone hour on Sunday mornings.

Therefore, God steps in to rearrange our lives in such a way that we must stop and focus upon Him, if only for a moment. C. S. Lewis describes the process like this:

> I am progressing along the path of life in my ordinary contentedly fallen and godless condition, absorbed in a merry meeting with my friends for the morrow or a bit of work that tickles my vanity today, a holiday or a new book, when suddenly a stab of abdominal pain that threatens serious disease, or a headline in the newspapers that threatens us all with destruction, sends this pack of cards tumbling down. At first I am overwhelmed, and all my little happinesses look like broken toys. Then, slowly and reluctantly, bit by bit, I try to bring myself into the frame of mind that I should be in at all times. I remind myself that all these toys were never intended to possess my heart, that my true good is in another world and my only real treasure is

Christ. And perhaps, by God's grace, I succeed, and for a day or two become a creature consciously dependent on God and drawing its strength from the right sources.[1]

It's humbling to think that we turn to God only when our life begins to disintegrate. Humbling and, unfortunately, accurate. In God's mercy, He helps us find time for Him by taking away the attraction of everything else that competes for our affections. He slows us down so that we can hear the Spirit's call and realize the true longing of our heart.

The Place of Suffering

God uses adversity to do more than get our attention. Adversity and suffering can bring about an intimate fellowship with God that cannot be experienced any other way. Remember that God doesn't end all suffering for Christians, but instead He shares it. I would like to take that premise a step further: There is a unique fellowship with the Lord that can only be found in the cauldron of suffering. Moreover, this is the closest, most intimate, most rewarding, and most difficult fellowship with God we will ever know. Being "close to God" doesn't insulate us from problems. In fact, the reverse is usually true: Problems lead us closer to God.

Paul never reached a lower point than when he was placed in prison for the final time. He knew the Roman authorities would soon kill him. The race was over; his battles had all been fought. Death was only days away. To make matters worse, he faced his most trying hour alone. He wrote Timothy saying, "At my first defense, no one came to my support, but everyone deserted me" (2 Timothy 4:16). Old friends deserted him; supposed Christians stabbed him in the back. Yet Paul could boldly proclaim, "The Lord stood at my side and gave me strength" (v. 17). God's presence became more than spiritual theory; it was tangible and real.

Paul's experience isn't unique. In our hour of greatest trial God comes and draws close to us. Look at your own life. When have you sensed the presence of Jesus Christ in a way that cannot be described with words? At what point has prayer seemed as natural as drawing a breath—a vital priority in your life? When could you sense the arms of God wrapping around you and carrying you through situations beyond your control? If you are like me, the answer is the same to all of the above. I'm closest to the Lord when I am going through trials.

This presents a great dilemma for all of us. Even though we know that God is nearest to us in times of suffering, we still long for those times to end. I find myself being caught in a paradox. I want to know the Lord; I want to walk in intimate fellowship with Him. But am I willing to say that I, like Paul, am willing to share in His sufferings to make this a reality? Our natural inclination is to regard misery as something totally negative, but Philippians 1:29 tells us that suffering for Christ is a gift of His grace. When bad things happen I usually begin looking for a way out. God uses them as a way of drawing close and spending quality time with me. Pain makes me want to shake a fist at heaven and scream out "why?", when in truth God is reaching down to draw me close to His side. I want to be close to Him; more than almost anything else I want to know Him intimately. The question I face is whether or not I am willing to pay the price to make that fellowship a reality.

God's promise to stay near our side doesn't insulate us from feeling alone and isolated. Let's face it, being a Christian can be a very lonely enterprise. Peter described us as strangers and aliens in the world. Though we may look like everyone else on the outside, Christ's presence in our heart makes us radically different. Our hopes, dreams, and expectations are all tied to our true home in heaven. While we travel in this life we can never be completely satisfied. The homesickness never goes away. Add to this the natural antagonism between the world and the church, and the result can leave us feeling very out of place, very homesick, very alone. In these moments we need more than knowing that God is near. We want someone we can touch and see, someone on our side who will assure us that we aren't alone. We need someone who will encourage us, cry with us, and walk along beside us. That is why God gave us the church.

GOD'S COMMUNITY: THE CHURCH

Volumes have already been written on the church. It's not my purpose to repeat their efforts. But it is impossible to write a travel guide for the journey of faith without including a section devoted to the church. In fact, this entire book needs to be understood within the context of a local church. We don't travel alone, although we often think that we do. The usual mental picture we draw of this trip consists of only two persons, me and Jesus. The poem "Footprints" popularizes this notion. In the poem a believer finds himself walking alone with Jesus down a lonely beach, the two sets of tracks becoming one when He stooped down to carry the believer through the most difficult part of the journey.

I like the point the writer of the poem is trying to make. As we've seen, there are situations we face as Christians that we could not survive if the Lord didn't carry us through them. But how many times in the Gospels do we see Jesus walking along with only one person? Never. He always worked with a group. That group was as small as two or as large as many thousands. Not everyone in the crowds that followed Him wanted to be His disciple. But those who did were grouped together into a diverse band made up of fishermen, zealots, and tax collectors. Some were hicks from Galilee; others were more cosmopolitan. Some had a strong religious background, whereas others like Matthew were as far from God as a first-century Jew could stray. If one of them looked back at the footprints of his journey with Christ, he'd find something closer to Pismo Beach on the Fourth of July than the solitary tracks of "Footprints." The members of this band of followers soon discovered that they not only needed Jesus, they needed one another.

This presents typical Americans with some problems. We don't like to admit that we need anyone. Rugged individualists founded our nation, and we work hard to carry on their tradition. We put fences around our yards to keep other people at arm's length, and we put walls around our hearts to keep anyone from getting close enough to discover our vulnerabilities. This idea also flies in the face of our usual notion of the church. Churches consist of buildings and denominations, programs and pews. People *go* to church once or twice a week to get their spiritual batteries recharged. We choose a church on the basis of what it has to offer, the quality of the preaching, the size of the choir, or the programs it has to offer our children.

The New Testament presents a very different picture. Christians don't *go* to church; we *are* the church. Church doesn't exist to serve me and my needs; rather, it's a place where I strive to become a servant. The church Jesus founded is all about people, not programs. As for denominations, He has a plan for every local body of believers, regardless of the name on the sign. The church is His body, His bride, His instrument for transforming the world. The members share something that will last forever: They have all been forgiven and transformed by Jesus' death and resurrection. This common experience makes us brothers and sisters, people who love one another in spite of our differences. There's more. The message of the New Testament consistently tells us that an integral part of our fellowship with the God we cannot see comes through these brothers and sisters in Christ we *can* see. Our relationship with God is inseparably linked to our relationship with other Christians. It is what keeps us from being alone in this world.

The Obligations of Community

The Bible is filled with commands directed to each of us that can only be fulfilled within the fellowship of other Christians. We are told to love one another (1 John 3:11–18), serve one another (John 13:1–17), encourage each other (Hebrews 10:24–25), rescue those who fall back into sin (Galatians 6:1), bear one another's burdens (Galatians 5:13–14; 6:2), pray together (Acts 2:42), and push one another on toward spiritual maturity (Ephesians 4:12–13). In addition, Jesus left some unfinished business that can only be done by the church as a whole. He established His church to go and make disciples of all the world (Matthew 28:19–20) and to reconcile people to God (2 Corinthians 5:17–21). The church should be a refuge for those who hurt, a place where anyone can find comfort and acceptance (2 Corinthians 1:3–4). As we gather together with other believers we also experience a prelude to what heaven will be like. The fourth and fifth chapters of the book of Revelation pull back the curtains of heaven and give us a glimpse of our eternal destiny. All the hosts of heaven gather around the throne of God to worship the Lord and the Lamb. When we gather with our brothers and sisters in Christ we join in the business of heaven as we praise and worship our Lord and King.

Of course, as you probably already know, there are no perfect churches. Most have hypocrites on the rolls, the pastor will usually find a way to disappoint you, and people often disagree and get mad at one another. We may be saints, but even the best of churches find ways to act rather unsaintly. The point is not to find the perfect church. Nor is it to find the church that best meets your needs. God's plan for you and me is for us to find a church where we can worship God, where we can serve, where we can use our gifts and talents for the glory of God, and where we can pour out our lives without expecting anything in return. I know that sounds rather out of date in our era of mega-churches and gospel malls. It's not much of a marketing strategy, but it does ring true with the words of the One who said, "The Son of Man did not come to be served but to serve and to give His life as a ransom for many." The local gathering of believers we call the church is the place where we can put these words into practice.

The Church's Value to God

We grow so accustomed to God's grace that we come to take all the benefits for granted. With time we even forget what it cost God to make this all possible, the death of His only begotten Son. It's incomprehensible that God would desire fellowship with you and me. It's almost scandalous to think that He would sacrifice His only Son to make it possible. But there was no other way. Our sin separated us from God and therefore had to be removed. Only the death of the guilty party could accomplish this while maintaining God's justice. Jesus became that guilty party as He took our guilt upon Himself in order to reconcile us to the Father. God's only motivation, His only reason for paying such a high price, is His incomparable love. First Peter 3:18 says it best, "For Christ died for sins once for all, the righteous for the unrighteous, to bring you to God." As I said at the beginning of the chapter, this is a mystery we can never fully comprehend.

NOTE

1. C. S. Lewis, *The Problem of Pain* (New York: Macmillan, 1962), 106.

Travel Log:

*1. How close are you to God at this moment? Look carefully at your relationship with Him over the past few weeks. How would you describe it? Are you strangers? Acquaintances? Old high school buddies who haven't seen one another in years? Intimate friends? Or somewhere in between?*_____

_____

_____

*Has there ever been a time when you were closer to God than you are today?*_____

*If so, what happened? How did you drift away?*_____

_____

*2. Most of us struggle from time to time with how to draw near to God. We discussed three ways: quiet times, corporate worship, and ministry. In which of these do you find the greatest delight?*_____

_____

*Which one presents the greatest challenge?*_____

*Does the amount of time you spend on each give an accurate picture of the importance you place on knowing God?*_____

_____

*What other ways do you use to go into the very presence of the Father?*_____

_____

*Is there a special place you've set aside for Him?*_____

_____

3. The whole idea of meeting with an invisible God can seem like a mystical, existential experience. Personally, I like to deal with the concrete, with things I can touch and see. That's where the church comes in. God designed our fellowship with one another to be a means of drawing close to Him. In fact, our relationship with other

Christians is a good barometer of our relationship with the Father. I didn't come up with this idea. John wrote of it long ago when he warned us, "Anyone who does not love his brother, whom he has seen, cannot love God, whom he has not seen" (1 John 4:20). Strong, convicting words.

*What kind of relationship do you have with other Christians?*_____
_____

*Do you meet together to pray and to worship?*_____

*Are you actively involved in a local church?*_____

*Have you dropped your guard so that you can love and be loved within your church family?*_____

It's not an easy thing to do. You have to risk being hurt. But the alternative is no choice at all.

Chapter Ten

IS THIS PLACE ON THE MAP?

So far we've traveled a long way. Maybe you're getting tired and are looking for a place to rest. This journey that takes a lifetime to complete demands a lot of energy. The Lord never leaves us to find our own way, but takes us by the hand to guide us. Times come when a fog settles down, and the path the Lord is blazing becomes obscure. We wonder if anyone knows where we are going, especially God. His guiding hand seems far away, and we question how He could lead us here. Other times we simply get tired of the trip. A lifetime is a long time and the journey of faith can be very slow and monotonous. We get bored with it all and are ready to move and do something else. And we often find ourselves choosing our own direction, giving in to our flesh and falling into sin. Any and all of these leave us feeling lost, stranded in a thick fog, unable to find our way back to where we think we are supposed to be. The adventure appears to be over. What do we do then?

Let's back up a little bit. Before we can explore what we need to do, we need to determine how we got into this predicament.

Many things can cause us to lose our way or to feel lost on the journey. The greatest perhaps is the frustration we often feel while trying to determine God's will for us personally. I think all of us would feel much more secure if the Lord led us the same way He did the children of Israel in the wilderness. Can you imagine having a pillar of cloud and fire leading you day after day? No need to worry and fret about which job to take or where to go to church. Look out the window at the pillar and there it would be, right before our eyes, God's will.

Unfortunately, although the pillar of cloud and fire disappeared when the Israelites entered the Promised Land, we're still in the wilderness of life, searching for God's direction. We want Him to guide us; we need to know His will in the decisions we face. Whom should I marry? Which job offer should I accept? Where should I live? What does God want me to do with my life? Everyone wrestles with these questions.

As followers of Jesus Christ we believe the Lord Himself will supply the answers. Our ears strain to hear His voice, and our eyes constantly scan the horizon, looking for a sign. Yet there are times when it seems that finding God's will is similar to discovering the lost ark of the covenant or the ashes of the red heifer. We know it must be out there somewhere, but where? We wonder why our questions go unanswered, why He doesn't give us an unmistakable sign. Sometimes we want to scream, "What do You want me to do now, God?!" But all we hear is silence.

Now, don't misunderstand me. I firmly believe God makes His plan for our lives crystal clear. Yet He rarely, if ever, reveals that plan in the same way He spoke to Peter in Acts 10. There we read of Peter having a vision of a huge sheet being lowered from heaven with all sorts of creepy, crawly creatures on it. The original language of the New Testament describes them in a way reminiscent of the Beverly Hillbillies' menu: bugs and lizards and strange birds. The sight of it nearly took Peter's appetite away (it was almost lunchtime). Then a voice thundered from heaven, "Get up, Peter. Kill and eat" (Acts 10:13).

"I don't think so, Lord," was Peter's response. "I've never eaten anything impure or unclean." *And I'm not about to start now*, he surely thought (see v. 14).

The voice thundered a second time, "Don't call anything

impure that God has made clean."

You would think that this would settle the matter for Peter. How much more of a definitive "word from the Lord" can you receive than to actually hear an audible word from the Lord? Unconvinced, Peter argued with God *three* times over this sheet full of disgusting creatures that God wanted him to eat. God soon made it clear that He was less concerned with the eating of lizards than He was with taking the gospel to the world. He made His will known: Peter was to go and preach to the Gentiles.

Problems arise and frustration sets in when we begin to think that Peter's experience is the normative way to discern God's will. Even a casual reading of the New Testament reveals that such conversations with the Lord were out of the ordinary and usually confined to a handful of people. Yet God was still able to communicate His will to first-century believers, and He continues to do so today.

THE ROAD MAP

The greatest embodiment of the revelation of His will can be found in black and white, in the pages of the Bible. The vast majority of the things God wants each one of us to do are written there for anyone to read. First Thessalonians 5:16–18 says that God's will is for us to "be joyful always; pray continually; give thanks in all circumstances." No fireworks, just practical, timeless directions. We also know that the Lord wants us to witness to the lost and to help people in need. Loving one another and forgiving one another are part of His will for our lives as well. Yes, the specifics for our individual lives can become obscure as we walk down the path of faith. But I believe that if we begin by doing the parts of His will we know—the parts He makes clear in His Word—the rest of it will fall into place.

Sometimes the worst part of searching for God's will is finding it. I think about a fishing trip I took with my stepfather when I was thirteen. Late at night the drag on my fishing pole began to sing as a large fish took off with my bait. I jumped out of my sleeping bag and fought the lunker as it swam down the muddy river. Finally I landed it and ran to the lantern to get a good look at my prize. To my dismay, all I had caught was a big, ugly, scaly carp. Some people may eat them, but where I grew up in Oklahoma, all they were good for was throwing on the bank for the raccoons.

I've found myself reacting to God's will for my life in the same way. He has led me down some paths that make me ask Him to show me the map; I'm convinced we had to be lost. In the first chapter we looked at the life of Jeremiah and found how his obedience to God led him to strange and exotic places, like the bottom of a well. We need to remember that faith doesn't guarantee happy endings, and obedience doesn't always lead to a place of comfort and blessing.

It didn't for Tony Senora. Tony pastors a church located atop the world's largest garbage heap, Smoky Mountain, outside Manila. Thousands of the Philippines' poorest people call this dump home, Tony and his wife and their four daughters among them. They survive by scavenging whatever food they can among the rotting garbage. Tony would love to move to the United States and live in a comfortable, suburban home. But he is convinced God wants him right where he is, giving his life to meet the needs of people everyone else has turned their backs on. "My heart belongs to the Lord and my plan is to help the squatter," Tony explains.[1]

I'm not eager to trade places with Tony Senora. The price he has paid to follow God's leadership is more than I ever want to pay. Yet I envy him. He's a rare individual, for only one so rare could be entrusted by the Father with a task so important. His fog is real, a smoke that never dies as garbage burns day and night. But atop Smoky Mountain he is in the center of God's will. The Lord often leads us to places we would rather not go, but once we get there, we find that there is no other place we would rather be.

THE NEED FOR REST

That's not to say that the journey of faith is a relaxing Sunday afternoon stroll through the park. It involves lots of hard work that leaves us exhausted. Elijah found this out. God revived the age of the miraculous through him, doing things unheard of since the days of Moses. Single-handedly he stood up to the apostate king Ahab and his wicked wife, Jezebel. The climax of his ministry came atop Mount Carmel when he challenged 850 of the queen's false prophets to prove once and for all who was truly God, the Lord or Baal. Jezebel's prophets cried out to their gods all day long, frantically praying, dancing and slashing themselves with knives, all to no avail. Then Elijah calmly stepped up to the Lord's altar, covered it with water and prayed down fire from heaven. The king stood by shocked and stunned. All the people were amazed and cried out, "The Lord—he is God! The Lord—he is God!" (1 Kings 18:39).

A few days later we find Elijah hiding in the desert, asking God to take his life. What happened? How could he go from standing alone for the Lord before an entire nation to wanting his life to end in so short a span? We find the answer in the way God reacted to Elijah's plight. He didn't strike His prophet dead. Rather, He told him to take a nap, a long nap, a nap of Garfield the cat proportions. Elijah hadn't lost his nerve; he had simply exhausted all his physical, emotional, and spiritual energy. He needed lots and lots of rest so that he could return to Israel and finish the tasks God had given him.

Most of us will feel like Elijah at some point. The path seems much too long and tiresome. It's as though we can't take another step. We'd like to find a place to stop and give up the fight. In that moment we feel very alone and very guilty, as though we're letting down God and everyone else who depends on us. The guilt may even keep us going for a short while, but not for long. Eventually, the fatigue builds up and our spiritual life comes to a screeching halt. Call it burnout or some other label, it is one of the darkest experiences we'll ever face as believers. And if it could happen to Elijah, a man so close to God that he didn't experience death but went directly to heaven, it can happen to me and you.

The temptation we face in that hour is to shake a fist toward heaven and abandon God. Satan doesn't help matters. He slithers nearby and begins to whisper that this whole Christianity thing is a fraud and it doesn't work. If it did, would you be feeling this way? I know what I'm talking about; I've been there. When I resigned my first pastorate to return to seminary, my wife and I were certain this step was God's will. He miraculously made that clear time after time. In spite of God's leadership, this step of faith plunged us into one of the greatest trials my family has ever faced. Lying awake in the dark early one morning in the middle of this time, I closed my eyes and pinched myself, hoping everything had been a bad dream and that I could go back to the place where I was before God messed up my life with His plan. Yet somewhere in the darkness something kept me going. That is, Someone kept me going. I discovered the Lord was at my side. Silently He told me, "Rest, Mark, you've been through a lot. Let Me take over now." Nothing had changed when I woke up. The situation that obedience had led me into remained as bleak as ever. Yet, slowly but surely, the Lord began to renew my strength and prove once again that "if we are faithless, he will remain faithful, for he cannot disown himself" (2 Timothy 2:13).

THE EXCITEMENT OF THE JOURNEY

Boredom also creates a fog along the path of faith. Boredom? How could anyone get bored in the great adventure of faith? Bunyan's pilgrim never got bored in *The Pilgrim's Progress*. Paul's life was anything but boring. And what about David? Excitement was his middle name. Surely the life of faith must be action-packed, a thrill ride with God, sort of a spiritual "Space Mountain."

If the life of faith is anything like an amusement park thrill ride, it usually comes closer to the wait in line than to the ride itself. Most of what we do as Christians is routine and ordinary. Parenting is like that. Cooking meals and changing diapers lack excitement. Life becomes routine (abbreviated: rut!). Godly parenting involves faithfulness and consistency, giving love so frequently that its recipients take it for granted. It lacks the thrills many of us seek, but the rewards are incomparable.

Ministry also becomes monotonous with time. I remember when God called me to preach—I couldn't wait to lead the world to Christ. But it didn't take long for my calling to become a job. Week after week I do the same sorts of things. There are sermons to prepare, couples to marry, problems to solve, buildings to construct. It hardly compares with being a Hollywood stunt man on the thrill-o-meter. Boredom often makes ministry difficult. Yet through it all I remind myself that God called me to do this work, and He continues to call me to be faithful. What a thrill it will be one day to step into heaven and see the fruit that God produced through me in what seemed to be dry periods.

Whether or not an individual's calling is to full-time ministry, everything a Christian does is to be done for the Lord. With time it will become monotonous. Boredom sets in and makes us think that we must have missed something along the way.

When you feel this way, don't worry that you must be strange. Be patient. The Lord supplies times along the way to refresh us and renew our enthusiasm. Even if the enthusiasm is lacking, remember this: We are walking by faith, not by sight or by feelings. It's not thrills we seek, but the Lord.

DISTRACTIONS AND GETTING LOST

To get a complete and honest picture of the journey of faith, we also need to look at a phenomenon that is all too common. Sometimes we get lost along the way. I don't mean that we lose our salvation or that the Lord abandons us. Even as Christians, as those who say we want to follow Jesus with our lives, we often choose to go our own way. We have a lot of names for the result: backslidden, out of fellowship with the Lord, not being quite as close to God as we used to be. However we describe it, the sad fact remains that we who have experienced God's gift of new life in Christ frequently fall back into sin.

The process starts slowly, with a gradual drifting away from God. It can start when a change in your work schedule causes you to stop having a daily time alone with God. Or you become so busy during the week that the weekend is your only time to get caught up on chores around the house. As a result, church attendance becomes less and less frequent until you find yourself completely out of the habit.

I think what usually causes us to drift off the path of obedience and faith is becoming distracted by something that catches our eye. We're like a child walking home from school who notices a butterfly flitting across her path. The beautiful orange and black wings and the delicate grace with which it flies capture her imagination. She decides to try to catch it. Paying no attention to where she is going, she jumps from flower to flower, desperately trying to grab hold of the butterfly, but always falling a second behind. After a while the insect goes up and out of sight and the child turns her attention back to the business at hand. As she looks around she realizes that she has no idea where she is or where home may be.

Even as adults we are susceptible to the occasional butterflies that cross our paths. Recently I found myself chasing after a new car butterfly. My family needed a larger car because we had gone from one child to three. I knew the old car was too small when my youngest daughter would reach from her car seat and take one sister's hair in each hand and pull as hard as she could toward the middle. Small trips to the grocery store consisted of constant screams from the back seat. The cross-country trek to the grandparents was unthinkable. So, I set out to buy a minivan. Six months and innumerable trips to car lots later we had our bigger car. In the process I had become a bit of an expert on minivans. I also found myself farther from God than I had been in years. It wasn't that I intended things to turn out that way. I hadn't fallen into any grave sins. Yet in the process of trying to find the right car at the right price with the right warranty and seating options I had lost sight of my first love. The Lord had become very distant, and I was lonely.

Lots of things distract us: friends, family, career, computers, sports, church. Even good things can become idols when they compete for the devotion that belongs to God and God alone. Perhaps that is why Christ said we had to take up our cross *daily* in order to follow Him. No one took up a cross in the first century except to die upon it. In the same way, we have to allow God to put our flesh and all of its attractions to death on a daily basis. Only then are we able to fully focus upon the Lord and follow Him without being distracted.

Choosing Our Own Route

All our sin cannot be explained away this cleanly. Most of it comes as a direct result of the clashing of two wills, God's and ours. Like Jonah, we often find God's will for our lives unacceptable, so we flee from Him. No one tricked Jonah into catching a ship to Tarshish. The life of a sailor hadn't captured his imagination. His only thought was to run as far and as fast from God as possible. The Lord said to go east to Nineveh, so he fled west. Even after being swallowed by a fish and finally preaching to the Assyrians, Jonah still grumbled against God's plan for his life.

Instead of rejoicing over what God had done through his preaching, he sat under the dried-up remains of a bush, bitter and angry, preferring death to life.

We don't always like the direction God takes our lives. What an understatement! As a result, we often join Jonah on board the ship to anywhere but here. I know a man who let his brother talk him out of going into full-time ministry because there wasn't enough money in it. Besides, they already had one preacher in the family. From that point forward this man's life has been spent running from one place to the next, looking for something to do with his life that will give him a sense of purpose without doing what God has called him to do.

Our will also clashes with God's when we want to do what He places off limits. The first man and woman had this trouble when they wanted to eat some fruit from a tree they were told to avoid. They ate it because they wanted to. Each one of us clashes with God over all sorts of forbidden things. The object of desire, like the forbidden fruit, isn't even the crucial issue. The heart of the matter is the eternal question, *Who is in control of my life, me or God?* Sin comes when I choose my way rather than God's. It is the very antithesis of faith.

We all find ourselves in this position. Occasionally our wills win out over God's. But our victory and freedom from His constraints soon result in bondage. What we thought would bring happiness and satisfaction can't deliver. The fun and excitement fade, leaving us lost and alone, wondering how we ever got into such a mess. "Big" sins like adultery aren't the only ones that end this way. All sin, from a little white lie to stealing a neighbor's car, breaks our fellowship with God. It corrupts our life and leaves nothing but pain and death in its wake, whether it's the death of a relationship or the death of our testimony.

Returned to Service

Mercifully, God doesn't leave us to wallow in the pit of our own making. Like a loving Father He does something to bring us back home. Hebrews says, "My son, do not make light of the Lord's discipline, and do not lose heart when he rebukes you, because the Lord disciplines those he loves, and he punishes everyone he accepts as a son" (12:5–6). The fact that God acts shows us how much He loves us. He cares too much about our welfare to leave us trapped in the deceitfulness of sin. Therefore, He disciplines us for our own good in order that we might share in His holiness.

The story of Jonah illustrates this point. God could have left Jonah on the boat and chosen another spokesman to go to Nineveh. Because He wanted Jonah to be part of the great revival He had planned for the capital city of Israel's archenemy, God went after him. He did anything and everything necessary to bring Jonah to his senses and have him obey the command to preach in Nineveh. Jeremiah spent his entire life preaching, without seeing one convert. Jonah preached one day and saw thousands turn to God, including the king of Assyria. The Lord didn't want him to miss out on that great privilege. God could have simply punished Jonah rather than disciplining him. He didn't have to send the great fish to swallow the wayward prophet; He could have just as easily let him drown in the Mediterranean. But He saved him in order to open Jonah's eyes to what He was doing and help him to see how great God's love was for him.

God's Use of Other People

Many times God's discipline comes through other people. David committed a series of sins that should have ended his life. He started with adultery and quickly sank to murder. By all rights he should have been put to death. Instead, God had mercy on the man after His own heart. Nathan the prophet went to David with a simple parable of a rich man stealing a poor man's lone sheep. The story so enraged the king that he declared, "As surely as the Lord lives, the man who did this deserves to die!" (2 Samuel 12:5).

Nathan calmly replied, "David, you are that man" (see v. 7).

Few things are harder than going to a friend who has sinned. I've had to do this several times but have never gotten used to doing it. The words stick in my throat, and I pray that God will open his eyes to his sin without my having to get involved. But as brothers and sisters in Christ, as fellow travelers on the journey of faith, we have an obligation to help those who stumble and fall. Paul commanded those who were spiritual in Galatia to restore those of their fellow believers caught in sin. But it must be done gently, each watching out for himself, for the person who is confronting never knows when the tables will be turned and he will be the one who needs to be restored.

The happy ending to the story of falling into sin is that there is hope on the other side. No one illustrates that better than Peter. He denied the Lord at the crucial hour when he was needed most, not once, but three times. Peter was convinced that it was over for him. After Christ rose from the dead Peter went back to Galilee and his fishing boats. Jesus followed him. And early one morning the risen Lord extended His invitation to Simon to once again become Peter, the rock, and to live a life that would end in glory to God. David also went from his darkest hour of sin to be used by God as the greatest king Israel ever knew.

There is hope for you even if you feel like you've blown your chance with God. You can still come home and be used by God. The way back isn't easy, however. Like the prodigal, you've got to leave the mess you've gotten yourself into—and the sin that took you there—and come back to the Father. The faith that started you on this journey is the same thing that brings you back, a faith that casts you totally on the goodness and mercy of God. He promises that if you will turn back to Him, He will forgive you and freely accept you back into the family.

Forgiveness doesn't mean all the consequences of sin are removed. But God will walk with us through whatever storms we have created for ourselves to use them for His greater glory.

NOTE

1. Michael Chute, "God's Plan for Smoky Mountain," *The Commission* 53, No. 6 (August 1990).

Travel Log:

*1. Do you struggle to know God's will?*_____
Life would be much easier if we could see some sort of
physical manifestation of His leadership, like the pillar of fire
that led Israel through the wilderness. Unfortunately, He extin-
guished the fire a long time ago. Yet, just as He led Israel, He still
leads you and me, only without the pyrotechnics. How has God giv-
en you clear directions in the past?_____

_____

*Where do you look as you search for His will?*_____

_____

*Perhaps the most important and challenging question we all wres-
tle with is whether we are willing to do anything God wants us to do.
Are you? Can you honestly say that you will go anywhere He leads?*

_____

*2. Has God ever led you to a place that left you wondering if He had
taken a wrong turn?*_____

*Go back to the first chapter and revisit Jeremiah at the bottom of a
well. Has His Spirit ever led you to places that seemed just as cold
and damp? The hardest part of the experience comes from knowing
that the bottom of the well is exactly where God wants you. What did
you say to Him during that experience?*_____

_____

*What was His response?*_____

_____

*How did God use you in the midst of the wrong turn, and what
lessons did He have for you there?*_____

_____

*3. I've tried to be very honest with you through these pages about
what you can expect in the uncommon adventure we call faith. It's
not a party or a yellow brick road to happiness. Times come when the*

*road stretches on forever. Have you ever run out of spiritual energy when you didn't think you could take another step?*_____

*What gave you the strength to go on?*_____

_____

*How did God revive and refresh you?*_____

_____

*Have you ever grown tired of the journey?*_____

*Have you ever come close to simply losing interest in the whole excursion?*_____

Don't worry, you're normal if you have. God's faithfulness keeps us going. If He left us to ourselves and our strength, none of us would make it to the finish line. Maybe you're going through one of those times right now. The best advice I can offer is this: Find a brother or sister who has walked with Christ for many years, someone you respect and trust, and talk to him or her about what you are going through. Chances are, he or she has walked that path and will be able to relate. Be honest, nothing held back. Together you can find your way back on track.

Chapter Eleven

THE
HOME
STRETCH

*T*here are a lot of unknowns as we travel with
Jesus. We don't know what tomorrow may hold;
we don't know how He may decide to use us today; we don't
know what the effects of yesterday's decisions may be. Yet we can
always be sure of where He is ultimately leading us: the gates of
heaven. The hope of spending eternity with Jesus is our one,
absolute certainty. It's the unspoken plot line the rest of our life's
story builds upon. We may not think about heaven every day, but
its hope always burns within us. Silently, quietly, it gives us the
strength to press on by assuring us that God has greater things
planned for us than what we find in this world.

This hope sets us apart from the rest of the world. We're different. In Jesus we know the end of the story line of history. Life
no longer lies before us like a dark, frightening expanse. Valleys
stretch out before us, but we can see the city that lies just beyond
the horizon. That's where we're going, and nothing will stop us!
We call it home, for we cannot be truly at home anywhere else.
God created us for eternity, not for the trappings of time and

space. We belong with Him, forever.

The anticipation of going home wells up within us until it erupts in song. From ancient hymns to contemporary Christian hits, there's nothing we love to sing about more. It's only fitting, since the book of Revelation tells us that heaven itself resounds with singing as the multitudes of heaven's host surround the throne of God with celebration.

WORTH SINGING ABOUT

Songs about heaven have a way of lifting our souls and setting our sights above the troubles of today. As this journey gets long and tiresome and the trials we face become unbearable, singing about what lies ahead in heaven's glory restores our joy. Charles Tindley captured this idea in his wonderful hymn, "When the Morning Comes."

Trials dark on every hand, and we cannot understand
All the ways that God would lead us to that blessed promised land;
But He'll guide us with His eye, and we'll follow till we die;
We will understand it better by and by.

Oft our cherished plans have failed, disappointments have prevailed,
And we've wandered in the darkness, heavy-hearted and alone;
But we're trusting in the Lord, and according to His Word,
We will understand it better by and by.

Temptations, hidden snares often take us unawares,
And our hearts are made to bleed for some thoughtless word or deed,
And we wonder why the test when we try to do our best,
But we'll understand it better by and by.

By and by, when the morning comes,
When the saints of God are gathered home,
We will tell the story how we've overcome;
We will understand it better by and by.

Most of us can relate to the troubles he describes. They dog our every step. Yet, knowing that heaven lies before us gives us the strength to endure. It also helps with the question of why trials surround us. We may never receive the answer in this life, but "we'll understand it better by and by."

The promise of heaven's glories also comforts us in times of agony and grief. Horatio Spafford discovered this promise to be more than words when he lived through the sudden death of his wife and three daughters. As the pain and grief weighed down upon him he penned these words:

When peace, like a river, attendeth my way,
When sorrows like sea billows roll;
Whatever my lot, Thou hast taught me to say,
It is well, it is well with my soul.

In the final stanza of this classic hymn he tells us how he could face such tragedy and still say, "It is well with my soul."

And, Lord, haste the day when the faith shall be sight,
The clouds be rolled back as a scroll,
The trump shall resound and the Lord shall descend,
"Even so"—it is well with my soul.

It is well because it isn't the end. The day God promised in the fifteenth chapter of First Corinthians is the lifeline that rescues us from the depths of sorrow. Without that promise the words of this hymn would be impossible.

PROMISE FOR THE JOURNEY

Perhaps heaven plays such a vital role in the songs of our faith because it summarizes what this journey of faith is all about. We've never seen heaven, nor has anyone died and come back to tell us what it is like. All we have is a promise, a promise from God that His Son is preparing a place for us and that He will soon come to take us there. That's it, that's all we have to go on. Now by faith we set out with Him in pursuit of the place He has prepared for us. We're following someone we cannot see to a place we've never been, a place we call home. Now our entire perspective on life is changed. The things we can see we consider to be temporary; the things we cannot see are permanent. All that we can attain in this life means nothing in the life to come. Death, the end of life as we know it, becomes a stepping-stone, a new beginning to a life that will never end. No wonder people call us crazy. It all seems ludicrous until you meet Jesus personally.

Of course no sane person prefers any of the alternatives to heaven. Mankind needs a hope that stretches beyond the grave. We want to believe that there is something more. Our minds recoil from the thought that all there is to life is what can be experienced now and that everything ends at death. Life would be a cruel joke, a dream that is forgotten in the morning as though it never occurred.

HUMAN PERCEPTIONS OF THE DESTINATION

No one wants to spend eternity in misery, in hell. People long for a place where all of life's miseries will be over. No more sickness, no more death, no more morning aches and pains—that's the kind of heaven we want to go to. We want a heaven filled with people we love. Most of us look forward to a giant family reunion in the sky. We'd like to see the mother or father who died before us, and we anticipate meeting the heroes of history and talking to them about their lives. It will be like a giant party where the food never runs out.

We also think of heaven as a place of unsurpassed luxury. The Bible itself speaks of heaven as a place where the streets are paved with gold and the gates are made of giant pearls. The houses are mansions that far exceed anything even Donald Trump could build. No desire will go unfulfilled. Everything we want will be right at our fingertips, without our even having to ask. Night will never fall, and sorrows will never come.

If this is heaven, then it would be little more than a bribe to persuade us to live a good life. Faith would be void of meaning; devotion to God would be nothing more than a means to an end. The point of heaven is none of the above. The streets of gold tell us less about heaven than they do about earth. On a scale of eternity, gold is worth little more than salt that has lost its savor, which Jesus tells us is good for nothing more than being thrown out into the streets to be trampled underfoot by men. The precious stones used in the construction of the heavenly city as described in the twenty-first chapter of Revelation are all in the foundation. No one pays any attention to the foundation once the city is built. It is hidden from view and quickly forgotten. The point of heaven is not even the ending of suffering and pain. Death, mourning, crying, and pain will all pass away without a trace. They won't leave any scars behind to remind us of how they once tormented us. As they pass away with the old order of things, they will soon be forgotten.

Heaven is more than paradise, far more than a giant family reunion in the sky. It is a place that revolves around a Person, the Lord God Himself. The true longing for heaven is the longing for Jesus. It caused Paul to write in Philippians 1:23–24, "I am torn between the two: I desire to depart and be with Christ, which is better by far; but it is more necessary for you that I remain in the body." True Christians share his dilemma. Our hearts' desire is to be with Jesus. We long to see Him face to face, to talk with Him, and to be with Him forever. Wherever He is doesn't matter as long as we get to be there too.

WEDDING ANTICIPATION

It's impossible to describe the depths of this desire to those who don't know Christ personally. The closest thing I can compare it to is the anxious anticipation a bride and groom experience as they wait for their wedding day. I remember how slowly time seemed to drag by as the days counted down toward that day. All I could think about was my bride-to-be. Her face was everywhere. What I wanted more than anything was to be with her and for the moment to never end. When a couple has to be separated for an extended period of time, the desire to be together becomes unbearable. Nothing matters but having the separation end and being together.

The New Testament describes you and me as the bride of Christ. Time and space have separated us from Jesus. Though we've never seen Him face to face, we love Him. We know Him by faith and we long to know Him by sight. The joy that awaits us is the joy of His embrace. No wonder heaven erupts in praise when that day finally arrives. Nothing can compare to the joy of that moment, a joy that will never fade. All that we have wanted will be ours at last. It is all found in one Person, Jesus. Those who go through life longing for something else could never be satisfied with what heaven has to offer, but we who follow Christ by faith could never be satisfied with anything less.

Heaven isn't just the end of the journey of faith; it's the culmination of everything God brings us through along the way. In the gates of glory all that God worked to bring about in our lives on earth will find its final and perfect completion. Our holiness will be completed when we finally stand before the Lord in glory. When our mortal body is clothed with immortality all the final traces of sin will be eliminated once and for all. We will finally be able to go into the presence of God without fear of death, for we shall be like Him, holy. All that will remain of sin will be a memory of what it cost God to remove it.

The growing pains of coming to maturity will also be over. We won't waver any longer between faith and doubt. One look at the face of Jesus will sweep doubt away forever. The short time of trials that served to refine and purify our faith will be over. They will give way to praise, glory, and honor as Jesus Christ is revealed. On that day we will be perfected once and for all. Throughout eternity our lives will testify to the wonderful grace, mercy, and power of God.

Even the time of serving God on earth will find its ultimate expression in heaven. The only change will be the task at hand. We'll have a new job to do. Once the last trumpet sounds, the work of taking the gospel to the world will be over. Don't worry, God has something else planned. The final chapter of the Bible tells us that we will serve Him and reign with Him forever. No wonder serving Him here on earth is so important. Only those who have discovered the joy of losing their lives to the Lord and serving Him here will be prepared to enjoy eternity.

EYES ON THE DESTINATION

We don't have to wait for eternity to be ushered in for the hope of heaven to change our lives. When this hope infiltrates our hearts it begins to adjust our thought processes, beginning with the way we see ourselves and our world. We don't belong here; it is not our home. Like travelers passing through the desert on their way to paradise, our stay here is temporary. We should not become attached to the things of this world, because they have no value in the world we're going to. They're little more than the blades of grass of early spring, which soon wilt and fade away under the heat of the summer sun.

Seeing our world from the perspective of the world to come sets us free from the materialism that has captured our society. We don't have to worry about what we will wear, where we will live, or the kind of car we drive. It's like worrying about the color of towels in a hotel room. They don't really matter, since our stay is so short. We are free to be generous, to give things away, for we know that our true possessions lie in heaven. This also helps us to keep the problems of our world in perspective. The importance of who sits in the White House pales in comparison to who sits on heaven's throne. No matter what may happen politically on earth, there's always stability in the place where our citizenship truly lies. Knowing this, we can keep our heads and follow the Lord no matter what our circumstances may be.

Knowing where we are going also encourages us along the journey of faith. Throughout this travel guide we've found that the Christian life can be filled with heartaches and troubles. But we know that at the end of it lies a true blessing, the crown of life God promises to those who love Him (James 1:12). Paul persevered through heartache and suffering because he knew that there was in store for him "the crown of life" which the Lord will award to all those who long for His appearing. Trials last but a short time in comparison to the eternity that God has planned.

Looking at the end of the journey also gives us a sense of purpose in what we are going through. Because Jesus is coming back for us, because we will spend all eternity in His presence, our labor now has meaning and purpose. The fruits of our work for the Lord are deposited in heaven's vault. No other pursuit can make that claim. Professional athletes who give up everything to succeed in their sport soon see all their hard work end in vain. Someone else breaks their records. Striving to succeed in business ultimately ends without profit. All the wealth and goods accumulated wear out or go to someone else when we die. Fame is fleeting, beauty is vain. All that remains at the end of our lives is what we have done for the Lord. Everything else is fleeting, worthless.

Jesus said that giving a cup of water in the name of the Lord reaps eternal benefits. I can't help but wonder how radically different our churches and our nation would be if we who claim to walk with Christ would put this principle into practice. Can you imagine what God could do through us if we would "seek first His kingdom and His righteousness"? How many people might come to know Christ if we cared more about laying up treasures in heaven than our own personal bank accounts? This isn't a whimsical thought, a dream of an ideal world that will never take place. God doesn't hope we will someday set our sights on heaven. He commands us to do it *now!*

Our heavenly hope gives us more than a new perspective on life; it radically changes our desires. Listen to Paul's words to the church in Corinth:

> Therefore we are always confident and know that as long as we are at home in the body we are away from the Lord. We live by faith, not by sight. We are confident, I say, and would prefer to be away from the body and at home with the Lord. *So we make it our goal to please him, whether we are at home in the body or away from it.* (2 Corinthians 5:6–9, italics added)

Longing to be at home with the Lord fills our heart with one goal in life, to please the Lord. How did Paul arrive at that conclusion? Listen to the next verse:

> For we must all appear before the judgment seat of Christ, that each one may receive what is due him for the things done while in the body, whether good or bad. (2 Corinthians 5:10)

When Christ returns we will all stand before Him and give an account for what we did with the gift of eternal life He gave us. The questions we'll answer will be simple and straightforward: Did you seek My kingdom over everything else? Did you go and make disciples of the nations? Did you feed the hungry and clothe the naked? Did you care for the sick and visit those who were in prison? Did you do what I left you here to do? I don't think we'll need a giant television screen replaying our life history to find the answer. We know, and so does the Lord.

Judgment and Rewards

Jesus Christ is the only foundation we can build our lives upon. We use our time, talent, and energy either for Him or for ourselves. First Corinthians 3 calls the former gold, silver, and precious stones; the latter are wood, hay, and stubble. The day of judgment is like a fire sweeping down on the structures we build. Everything done for the kingdom of God endures, and we receive our reward. Everything else flashes into flame and soon disappears in a cloud of smoke. We won't lose our salvation, only the reward God had in store for us.

It's a sobering thought, especially when we consider that the crucial issue is not what we do but *why* we do it. The definitive chapter on love, 1 Corinthians 13, tells us that we can speak of the mysteries of heaven with the greatest eloquence, but it is worthless if we lack love. Our bodies can be handed over to death in a supreme act of sacrifice, but if it comes out of pride rather than love, it is all for naught. Even if we have faith, such faith like the world has never seen so that mountains move at our command, it means nothing without love. God searches the thoughts and intentions of our heart. Only what is done out of humble love and submission to Him matters.

What then of the rewards of heaven that Paul and the other New Testament writers spoke of? We find many references to crowns that will be given in heaven to those who are faithful. Paul compared himself to an athlete striving toward a victor's crown that lasts forever. Are our motives wrong if we copy Paul's example and strive for a heavenly trophy?

Working for Rewards

Two parables in Matthew's gospel give us our answer. The first is the parable of the sheep and the goats. On the day of judgment the Lord will separate the nations like a shepherd separates sheep from goats. The sheep, those who are righteous, are commended for putting the love of Christ into action. They fed the hungry, cared for the poor and sick, visited prisoners. What I find surprising is their reaction to the Lord's praise, "When, Lord? When did we do all these things to You?" (see Matthew 25:37–39). Their actions were such a natural, everyday part of their lives that they didn't give a thought to actually being congratulated for their works. I get the impression that the recognition is a little embarrassing, as though they would prefer to remain anonymous.

The second parable is the story of three stewards who were entrusted with their master's fortune while he was away on a trip. Two of the three used what they had received to multiply their master's goods. Neither had been specifically told to do this, nor were they promised any kind of reward. Their only motivation seems to be their desire to please their master. If so, their greatest reward came in six words, "Well done, good and faithful servant!" (Matthew 25:21).

Matthew places these two parables together in the same chapter, so that they are to be understood in the same context. As servants of the Lord, our greatest desire is to please the One we love. All the good works we could accomplish in a lifetime aren't meant as a bribe to try and buy our way into His good graces. Rather, they're acts of gratitude, motivated by love. As the parable of the sheep and goats demonstrates, with love as our motivation, the specific acts soon become natural. We hardly think about ourselves and what we have done. The ultimate reward we seek is to please the One who saved us.

As for the crowns, the fourth chapter of the book of Revelation tells us that we will cast them at the foot of heaven's throne as an act of gratitude and worship. How can we take any credit? All that we are and all that we do we owe to God's grace.

I don't know about you, but I can't wait for the journey to end and eternity to begin. The joy we will feel when we see Jesus for the very first time will never end. All the thrills and joys of this world last but a moment, but heaven's moment will never end.

When we've been there ten thousand years,
Bright shining as the sun,
We've no less days to sing God's praise
Than when we first begun.
Maranatha, Lord come!

Travel Log:

1. We've talked a lot about expectations in this book—what we expect from God when we follow Him by faith, what we expect from Him when we pray. As we turn our thoughts toward the ultimate prize, heaven itself, what do you expect to find there?_____

_____

What are you looking forward to that makes you want to spend all eternity in this place?_____

_____

Now compare your answers with what you just read. Which captivates your imagination—the place or the Person who is the centerpiece of it all?_____

_____

2. Has the hope of heaven changed your perspective in this life? How?_____

_____

I want you to think about more than how the assurance of going to heaven takes away the fear of death. Look at your lifestyle. What do you find that reflects a heavenly outlook on life?_____

_____

In the final analysis, all that really matters are those things done for the kingdom of heaven, no matter how small or how great. As you examine your own priorities, how important is the kingdom of heaven in your day-to-day life?_____

_____

How has it affected your desires?_____

_____

How has it changed your daily activities?_____

_____

*3. I enjoyed writing this chapter more than any other. I hope that reading about what lies ahead of us at the end of the journey gives you a renewed sense of excitement and joy. To finally see the Lord face to face—can anything compare to the joy that moment will bring? When do you find your thoughts skipping ahead to the joy that awaits us?*_____

_____

*What songs turn your thoughts toward home?*_____

_____

_____

*How has this hope given you comfort and encouragement?*_____

_____

_____

Chapter Twelve

STEPPING
OUT ON
FAITH

I am a meticulous traveler. Trips are more than jumping in a car and driving from Point A to Point B. I like to pore over the atlas weeks in advance and plot each and every leg of the journey. I select the places we'll stop for meals and bathroom breaks, carefully measure the mileage between each, and compute the driving time required to get there. Then I make an agenda that shows the entire trip on paper, with every detail accounted for. Even after doing all this, one thing must still be done. Looking over maps and making grand plans doesn't get me from Indiana to Oklahoma until I load my van with everything from luggage to our cocker spaniel and make the drive. Seldom do trips go according to schedule. They usually have several surprises waiting along the way.

Through the pages of this book we've been looking at the atlas for the journey of faith. We plotted the many goals on the way to our ultimate destination and explored the highways we must travel. From start to finish, we have a general idea of where faith will lead us. There's only one thing left to do: Make the trip.

It's time to step out on faith and follow the Lord Jesus Christ as He leads us through the unmapped territory of the journey of faith.

Wait a minute! Didn't I just contradict myself? How can the journey go through unmapped territory, in light of the previous eleven chapters? The territory ahead of us is uncharted because no one has taken the exact path we'll travel. Oh, there may be many who have faced the same trials, the same crossroads and decisions. But we see the lives of other people in a completely different perspective than we see our own. Our own pain is magnified, that of others is minimized. The choices we face are harder than other people's. While we can empathize with others, *our* journey seems unique. It's unmapped territory because *we* have never been this way before. Only along the journey do we begin to learn from those who have gone before us and appreciate the trail they have blazed.

JOURNEYING FAITH

If we knew everything God had in store for us, faith wouldn't be required. If there weren't any surprises awaiting us, we would not need to rely upon God alone. If we knew all the places God planned to take us, most of us wouldn't make the trip. Jesus invites us to take a journey with Him. The thought is both exciting and frightening. Like Peter climbing out of the boat on a stormy sea, we set out by faith. I can't imagine the degree of trust Peter had in Jesus to believe he could actually walk on water. (Keep in mind that the other eleven disciples stayed in the ship.)

We go through the same thing. Jesus stands before us and calls out to us. Only when we truly believe that He is trustworthy and His offer is legitimate will we take the first steps toward Him. The story doesn't end here. Faith not only gets us out of the boat, but it keeps us going as the storm wails around us. We have to live by faith in order to complete the journey.

What does it mean to live by faith? Three times the New Testament quotes Habakkuk saying, "the righteous man will live by his faith." How? Before answering this, let's back up a little and recall what faith is. The faith that moves us to accept Jesus as our personal Savior is the same faith that we need to go through the lifelong journey He has in store for us. It's not a mystical force that makes God act on my behalf or a magic pill that causes every trouble to disappear.

Biblical faith is my *active* response to a sovereign Lord who loved me so much that He gave His only Son for me. As a result, an ordinary man can enter into an extraordinary relationship with God for all eternity. Believing in Him means entrusting Him with my life, even when reason cries out to do otherwise. To believe is to obey, to drop everything else and follow Jesus Christ. God is faith's one and only object. Everything else fades out of view. The Scripture also calls faith a gift that God bestows upon us. It doesn't originate in our hearts, but in the heart of God.

Living by faith begins with losing my life to God, surrendering my will to His. In a very real sense, to claim Jesus as my Lord means to give Him absolute control over my life. Jesus Himself said, "If anyone would come after me, he must deny himself and take up his cross daily and follow me. For whoever wants to save his life will lose it, but whoever loses his life for me will save it" (Luke 9:23–24). At first this seems like a radical idea, as though we are giving up a lot to follow Jesus. Lose my life? What could be more difficult?

When we see our lives from God's perspective, it becomes less difficult than it seems. We need to return to the start of the story in the Garden of Eden. God warned the first couple that the penalty for disobedience was death. The wages of sin remain the same today and throughout time. Yet Adam and Eve didn't drop dead the moment they ate the forbidden fruit. Current members of the human race don't die the moment they violate God's law. We can say that death refers only to spiritual separation from God or to the eternal penalty of sin beyond the grave, but I think that is too narrow. If the wages of sin is death, then everyone who commits even one act of sin deserves to die at the very instant of transgressing God's law. The fact that He allows us to continue living is an act of His grace. We forfeited life, but by His grace God gives it back to us. This is true both for believers and non-believers, for saints and pagans alike. Physical life is a gift from God.

Therefore, when Jesus calls me to lose my life and follow Him, He is asking me to give up something that doesn't even belong to me. I owe my life to Him. Although I think I'm in control of myself, I'm really not. I don't know what tomorrow will bring. My ability to control even my own future is limited at best.

In a very real sense, all of us are prisoners of forces outside our control. The place and time of our birth, our parents, our race—all of these were decided for us. As we grow older our illusion of sovereignty begins to fade. Circumstances and physical limitations give us little freedom in many of the choices we make. Even when we stand up and assert ourselves, we find scores of others doing the same. The world isn't big enough for 5 billion sovereigns.

FREEING FAITH

Faith sets you and me free from this pitiful cycle. When I lose my life to Jesus Christ I am losing it to One who transcends time and space. Circumstances don't govern His actions. He is in charge of *all* circumstances. Only when I surrender my life by faith will I be fully free to be all that God had in mind when He created me. I can confidently say, "Thy will be done," for I know that He has a will, a plan, just for me: "For we are God's workmanship, created in Christ Jesus to do good works, which God prepared in advance for us to do" (Ephesians 2:10). Jesus does not want merely to come into my life; He demands absolute control. He is Lord. Living by faith begins with surrendering to His lordship.

Losing my life to Christ takes me into the practical world of obedience. In the Sermon on the Mount Jesus told His audience that claiming Him as Lord means nothing apart from doing what He says. It only makes sense. All of us live under someone's authority, whether it's a parent, the government, or an employer. No one would last very long on a job if he refused to do what his boss told him to do. Our government locks up people who stubbornly refuse to obey its laws. We know how to submit to earthly authority, by obedience. The same applies to heavenly authority. If Jesus is Lord, He must be obeyed.

Many of us associate obedience with a list of negatives. I once heard a man instruct a fourteen-year-old boy in a juvenile detention center that Christians "don't smoke, don't chew, don't cuss, don't chase women, and don't go to rock-and-roll concerts."

The frightening thing is that this man truly believed this was all there is to being a Christian. He's not alone. From time to time all of us think of obeying Christ as nothing more than saying no to the flesh and avoiding sin. We compile a list of things a Christian does and does not do. Spiritual people keep the list.

The problem is that all of this is wrong. Faith brings us into an intimate, personal relationship with God. Lists do not. It is possible to do everything on our lists and still fail to walk in obedience to God. The Pharisees fell into that trap. They specialized in keeping the law, going so far as to add more regulations to make the law more rigid. If spirituality came through lists, the Pharisees would have been the most spiritual of all. But Jesus did not commend them; He called them to task for keeping the letter of the law while ignoring its heart. True obedience transcends lists and forces us to get to know God and to learn how to listen for His voice. It opens our eyes to the dynamic nature of the Bible, living letters from One who loves us. As we hear His voice, we act. As we see Him working, we join Him and become part of His eternal plan.

From time to time, God takes our obedience to new heights. Rare occasions will come when God gives us the privilege of putting all that we say we believe into action. He lets us live out the sermons we preach (all of us preach to others, though most don't have a formal pulpit) and the clichés we offer to others in their times of distress. We tell others to trust God and He will provide all their needs, or we say that the color of a person's skin doesn't matter in Christ. We deliver our messages so often we lose track of where we preach them. God lets us discover whether in fact we believe what we say by moving us into a position where we have to put what we say into practice. He allows everything we depend on for financial security to be taken away, or He providentially causes our path to cross with people outside our normal comfort zone. Obedience means putting our faith on the line and into action, even when it would be more natural to do otherwise.

ONLY FAITH

This moves us to another aspect of living by faith. When we decide to follow Christ we give up all other options. There is no

Plan B. We've already looked at how difficult the journey may become. Times will come when we will wonder if God knows exactly what He is doing or when the outcome of trusting Him is less than we desired. Real faith leaves us no other option than to continue to follow Him, regardless of the consequences.

We all know the story of Shadrach, Meshach, and Abednego and how God rewarded their faith by delivering them from Nebuchadnezzar's fiery furnace. These three men refused to fall down and worship the massive statue of the king, and they were tossed into a blazing oven. Their story had a happy ending. But they took their stand for God not knowing what the outcome would be. They infuriated the king by declaring,

> If we are thrown into the blazing furnace, the God we serve is able to save us from it, and he will rescue us from your hand, O king. *But even if he does not,* we want you to know, O king, that we will not serve your gods or worship the image of gold you have set up. (Daniel 3:17–18, italics added)

Shadrach, Meshach, and Abednego only had two options: Trust God and possibly die, or abandon Him and worship a false god. Plan B was no option at all. They chose the fire, convinced that God could deliver them, but willing to face the consequences if He did not. We may never face as dire a situation as these three men in Babylon, but the principle they lived by still applies to us. Following Christ, living by faith, means turning our back on all other options and trusting Him absolutely.

I find this to be both frightening and exciting. Part of the difficulty of living without a Plan B is not fully understanding what God has in mind for Plan A. I want to commit my entire future to Him, but I would also like to know what He plans to do with it. If He told me in advance, faith would no longer be needed. Living by faith means entrusting everything to Him and walking away from any safety valves we might need if God doesn't come through.

If that kind of dogged determination and commitment depended on me and my strength, I would give up right now. It's beyond me. That's the point. Faith moves us beyond ourselves to a place where we must depend upon God. Ephesians 2:8–9 assures us that faith itself comes from God as a gift. Left to our-selves, we would never entrust our lives to Him. Our faith flows out of God's faithfulness.

God moves this gift out of the heavenlies and into the grim world of reality through His Holy Spirit. Jesus promised to send His Spirit as a comforter and counselor so that we wouldn't be left alone in this world. Through the Spirit, God makes His pres-ence known to us on a daily basis. Living by faith means allowing the Holy Spirit to fill us—to take control of our lives—and fol-lowing His leadership. Apart from Him we will never endure. Through Him we will never fail.

An Example of Faith

Stephen is an example of the possibilities of what God can do in us when we are filled with the Spirit. The book of Acts gives few details about this man, except to describe him as "full of faith and of the Holy Spirit" (6:5). He boldly proclaimed the gospel to all who would listen (a characteristic of being filled with the Spirit), and it got him into trouble with the religious authorities. Skeptics came to argue, but none of them could stand up against the wisdom the Spirit gave him. Finally, the Jews ran out of patience. Their anger boiled over and they dragged him before the Sanhedrin. Through it all Stephen stayed calm, his face like the face of an angel. He answered all their charges and confident-ly showed how the Old Testament pointed to Jesus and declared Him to be the Messiah. It was more than the Jews could stand. They covered their ears, screamed at the top of their lungs, and stoned him to death. Through it all, Stephen's countenance was like the face of an angel as he stepped out of this existence and into the presence of God.

One phrase occurs over and over in the story of Stephen: He was filled with the Holy Spirit. We will probably never go through anything remotely as dramatic as Stephen's experience. That's not the point. Living for Jesus in the midst of a sinful world pushes us beyond our limits, but not beyond God's. The personal presence of His Spirit in our lives makes walking by faith possible. His gentle voice and constant encouragement keep us moving along the path. His boldness and wisdom allow us to do things we would have never thought possible. Everything is possible when we believe and walk in the power of His Spirit.

The Holy Spirit also adds a dynamic dimension to the walk of faith. He fills it with joy. All this talk of martyrs and commitment can lead us to believe that the Christian journey is supposed to be somber and serious. As we have seen, it does have its share of sorrow. Yet Jesus said that He came that we might have life and have it abundantly. In Him we find life the way God meant it to be from the beginning of time, life lived in close fellowship with Him. He never intended faith to be a spiritual Ironman Triathlon, a grueling test of endurance. Living by faith means living with real joy that transcends our circumstances.

Joyous Faith

The joy of the journey of faith comes from the presence of God. David knew this as he wrote to the Lord in Psalm 16:11, "You will fill me with joy in your presence." Later he wrote that God "put a new song in my mouth, a hymn of praise to our God" (Psalm 40:3). The closer we draw to God, the greater the joy. He is our strength, our song. His joy is indescribable and incomprehensible.

Joy is also a choice. That's where faith enters in. Throughout Scripture, in both the Old and New Testaments, we are commanded to rejoice. Paul told the church in Thessalonica to "be joyful always; pray continually; and give thanks in all circumstances." The Philippians were repeatedly told to "rejoice in the Lord." What I find amazing is the fact that Paul wrote these words from prison! In the dark confines of a Roman dungeon Paul could confidently say, "Rejoice in the Lord! It is no trouble for me to write the same things to you again, and it is a safeguard for you" (Philippians 3:1). Over the past ten years I've visited some fifteen prisons in four states as a volunteer with the Bill Glass prison ministry team. From a minimum security unit without a fence, to death row in Huntsville, Texas, I've talked to scores of inmates and become acquainted with life behind bars. I'll let you in on a little secret. There isn't a prison in America that I would like to visit permanently. Conditions are dehumanizing and degrading. And our prison system is a country club compared to the conditions Paul faced. Yet he could still say, "Rejoice in the Lord." Amazing!

Living by faith means choosing to rejoice. By faith we pursue God's will and happiness simultaneously. Joy doesn't depend on our circumstances, but on viewing our lives from God's perspective. This isn't optional. We'll never survive the trip without choosing by faith to rejoice in every circumstance. Joy also makes our faith attractive to those around us who struggle in a cruel world. It's the difference that sets us apart from those who have no hope and makes them want what we have found.

COSTLY FAITH

Very few are willing to face the hardships of this life of faith. Yes, God gave His Son to die for the sins of the world. And, yes, whosoever will may come and drink from the water of life Jesus offers. But most people don't care for the package deal Christ offers. Eternal life comes in exchange for our lives. Few are willing to make the trade. Even many of those who claim to be Christians really don't want to set out on the kind of journey biblical faith leads to. We may want inner peace or deliverance from guilt; we definitely want to avoid hell at all costs. The real question is, are we willing to take up our cross and follow Jesus?

Jesus made His demands very clear to those who would be His disciples. John records a strange event in the sixth chapter of his gospel. Huge crowds thronged to Jesus everywhere he went. His popularity was soaring to new heights. That is, until the crowds began to learn what it meant to follow Him. As they listened to Jesus invite them to share in His cross, many of them began to grumble among themselves, "This is a hard teaching. Who can accept it?" Rather than temper His words, Jesus went even further. He claimed to be the Son of Man who came down from heaven. If His words were true, the logical implication was that all who believed them must submit to Him. Most wanted no part of that. Verse sixty-six of the sixth chapter of John records, "From this time many of his disciples turned back and no longer followed him."

I am a pastor, and most of my close friends are pastors. I know how I react when people start leaving the church. It deeply disturbs me. My mind begins to race, wondering what I have done wrong. Although I don't run after all who leave, I do try to reconcile people and bring them back into the fellowship. Jesus did not do any of these things. Instead, He turned to the Twelve, the handful that remained, and asked them, "You do not want to leave too, do you?" (v. 67). I would be wringing my hands, wondering why attendance had dropped, but Jesus gave those who remained a chance to leave.

Peter's response to Jesus is timeless. It summarizes what it truly means to walk by faith. "Lord, to whom shall we go? You have the words of eternal life" (v. 68). The journey of faith is only for those who have come to that conclusion. As long as we believe there are other options, we'll take them. The rich young ruler wanted eternal life, but he wasn't willing to give up everything he owned to find it. He went away sad, no doubt trying to figure out some alternative to Jesus. In the parable of the sower and the seeds, only one of the four kinds of soil persevered and bore a crop resulting in eternal life. The other two that had sprung up abandoned Jesus for something temporal.

The adventure of faith is only for those who, like Paul, have taken everything they own and everything they hope to achieve and found that it cannot compare to Jesus Christ. Paul told the church in Philippi that everything else is rubbish—stinking garbage—in comparison to knowing Christ. He is more than a path to heaven, more than a quick fix to the problems of life. Jesus offers us life, real life, eternal life, lived in fellowship with Him. What about you? Are you willing to leave everything behind and set out on this uncommon adventure?

"Take up my cross and follow me,"
I heard my Master say;
"I gave My life to ransom thee,
Surrender your all today."

He drew me closer to his side,
I sought His will to know,
And in that will I now abide,
Wherever He leads I'll go.

It may be thro' the shadows dim,
Or o'er the stormy sea,
I take my cross and follow him,
Wherever He leadeth me.

My heart, my life, my all I bring
To Christ who loves me so;
He is my Master, Lord, and King,
Wherever He leads I'll go.[1]

NOTE

1. Words and tune (Falls Creek), B. B. McKinney, 1936. Copyright 1936, renewed 1964 Broadman Press: Nashville. Used by permission.

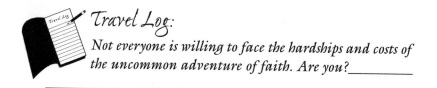

Travel Log:

*Not everyone is willing to face the hardships and costs of the uncommon adventure of faith. Are you?*_____

_____

I closed with a song, "Wherever He Leads, I'll Go." Can you honestly say that this is true for you? _____

_____

*Jesus gave His disciples a choice as the crowds were turning away. He asked them, "What about you, do you want to leave also?" As you gaze down the path at all God has in store, both good and bad, do you want to journey on or turn back?*_____

_____

*Are you willing to leave everything behind to follow Him?*_____

You might want to write a prayer to Him below, telling Him of your commitment. Sign and date it.

_____

_____

_____

_____

_____

_____

_____

_____

_____

_____

_____

_____

Moody Press, a ministry of Moody Bible Institute,
is designed for education, evangelization, and edification.
If we may assist you in knowing more about Christ
and the Christian life, please write us without obligation:
Moody Press, c/o MLM, Chicago, Illinois 60610.